IMAGES
of America

DAVENPORT

D1738290

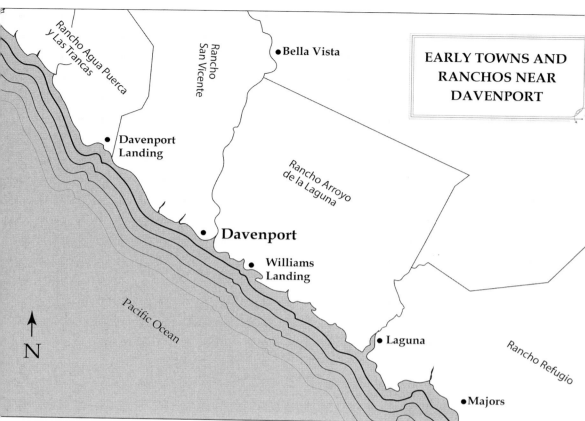

EARLY TOWNS AND RANCHOS NEAR DAVENPORT. This map shows the towns and landings that once surrounded Davenport. Also included are the pre-1850 Mexican land grant boundaries. Davenport is approximately 60 miles south of San Francisco, just north of the Monterey Bay. It is the only town left on the sparsely populated Santa Cruz County North Coast. (Courtesy of Sage Lee.)

ON THE COVER: THE HARVEY LINES. Open-air vehicles traveling from Santa Cruz to Pescadero stop for a photograph in front of the Ocean View Hotel in 1914. (Courtesy of Alverda Orlando.)

To Mary Jo & Val Belli
Enjoy! Alverda

IMAGES
of America

DAVENPORT

Alverda Orlando

Sally I—

Alverda Orlando, Sally Iverson,
and Ed Dickie

ARCADIA
PUBLISHING

Published by Arcadia Publishing
Charleston, South Carolina

Printed in the United States of America

Library of Congress Control Number: 2019949976

For all general information, please contact Arcadia Publishing:
Telephone 843-853-2070
Fax 843-853-0044
E-mail sales@arcadiapublishing.com
For customer service and orders:
Toll-Free 1-888-313-2665

Visit us on the Internet at www.arcadiapublishing.com

This book is dedicated to the pioneers and residents of Davenport
who shared their stories and inspired this project.

CONTENTS

ACKNOWLEDGMENTS

The authors would like to give special thanks to the following people and institutions for their help: Marla Novo and staff from the Museum of Art and History in Santa Cruz; Luisa Haddad, University of California, Santa Cruz (UCSC) Library Special Collections and Archives; Lucia Orlando, UCSC Research Support Services; Dennis Copeland, Monterey Public Library, California History Room Archives; Hui Lan Huang Titangos, Santa Cruz Public Library; Lud and Barbara McCrary, Big Creek Lumber Company; Kathleen Aston, Marisa Gomez, and staff at Santa Cruz Museum of Natural History; Satish Sheth, manager/vice president of Cemex; and Ken Kaanagaard and the Cemex crew.

We also extend our gratitude to current and former North Coast residents and others for their support: Fred Bailey, Noel Bock, Jim Cochran, Marvin del Chiaro, Cindi Escobar, Ross Eric Gibson, Josie Celebrado Gilbert, Leon Gregory, Brent Haddad, Steve Hicks, John Holbert, Steve Homan, Kris Houser, Jack and Arlene Licursi, Rebecca Lundberg, David Lundberg, Mike Luther, George Majors, Marcia McDougal, Allan McLean, Patty Morelli, Eleanor O'Connor, Frank Olympio Jr., Maria Olympio, Cheri Perez, Marion Pokriots, Kristen Raugust, Jeanine Scaramozzino, Amanda Trujillo, Michelle Vuckovich, Mark Wennberg, Derek Whaley, and Norma Wilson.

Special recognition is due to our exceptional historical analysts: Mark Hylkema, Frank A. Perry, Robert W. Piwarzyk, and Stan Stevens, who also provided indexing for this book.

The authors are deeply indebted to Sage Lee for map design and edits, Chacko Kuruvilla for edits, and Daisy Olazabal for research and organizational assistance.

This book was made possible in part by the generous support and assistance of the Santa Cruz County History Forum through the Dolkas/Mertz award and the expertise of individual members Traci Bliss and Randall Brown.

Unless otherwise noted, all images appear courtesy of Alverda Orlando. In this book, the term "North Coast" applies to the coastal areas from Point Año Nuevo to the city of Santa Cruz. The following abbreviations are used: Santa Cruz Museum of Art and History (MAH), the Coast Dairies and Land Company (CDLC), and Trust for Public Land (TPL).

INTRODUCTION

Davenport is situated along a beautiful stretch of the central California coast, 10 miles north of the city of Santa Cruz. Presently, the little town is a cozy spot where tourists and locals alike enjoy hidden beaches, surf, bike, and shop, or simply sit back and take in the expansive Pacific Ocean views. This area is also home to people who, like the land itself, are set apart. Some North Coast residents live and work on nearby farms. Others build their lives in the gentle hills and canyons or in the small communities that cling to the old Coast Highway. The coast holds historic communities such as Swanton, Laguna, Davenport Landing, and Bella Vista; places that at one time were thriving outposts, but are now just obscure names on a map. There are also a few "State of Mind" settlements—communities with unofficial, but commonly known, names—with homes but no conveniences sprinkled throughout, like Bonny Doon and Last Chance Road. Local residents must travel to Santa Cruz or other nearby cities to find grocery stores, clinics and hospitals, high schools, movie theaters, and other necessities.

For thousands of years, indigenous people have made the central coast their home. The land near Davenport was populated by the Cotoni (pronounced "koto-ne") people. Their world was vastly different from the one we see today. Early explorers were amazed at the area's large herds of elk, antelope and deer, bears by the thousands, flocks of ducks and geese, and a wide variety of other creatures. The Spanish mission era, 1769–1822, brought about abrupt changes for California's native population. Members from the Cotoni tribe were forcibly removed from their villages and brought to Mission Santa Cruz, where they joined other tribes from the region. Native people of the region and across the country were relegated to the lowest social order of the new society. Inside the mission walls, many native people died from disease and poor nutrition. The Cotoni were decimated, but some members survived and blended into Spanish, Mexican, and American cultures. Today, the Amah Mutsun Tribal Band, among others, represents the native people who lived in this area.

In 1821, Mexico achieved independence from Spain. Over the next decade, according to the new laws, the missions were secularized. Mission-owned lands were converted into large land grants and sold to private citizens. These ranchos relied heavily upon native labor, and indigenous culture continued to erode as the native people assimilated into their new environment. The year 1848 marked the end of the Mexican-American War, which resulted in the United States acquiring the present-day states of Arizona, Nevada, New Mexico, Texas, and California, and parts of western Colorado and southern Utah. As part of the Land Act of 1851, the United States agreed to honor the landholdings of Mexican citizens but forced the burden of legal proof on them. By the time the boundaries were approved, sometimes over two decades later, the court costs and fees were so high that landowners were often forced to sell to Americans or squatters already on the land.

The land along the North Coast of Santa Cruz County, including the present-day town of Davenport, is situated on three former Mexican land grant ranchos. A claim of 4,421 acres for Rancho Agua Puerca y Las Trancas was filed with the Public Land Commission in 1852. The neighboring 10,803-acre Rancho San Vicente land grant was patented to Blas Escamilla (also noted as Escarillo), and the 4,418-acre Rancho Arroyo de la Laguna land grant was patented to Gil Sanchez. (See map opposite title page.)

Around 1851, Capt. John Pope Davenport, a whaler by trade, was hauling fresh fruit to California. As he passed Monterey Bay, he noticed an abundance of whales traveling along their migratory

7

route. In 1869, Davenport moved his family to a small inlet 12 miles north of Santa Cruz. Here he built a 450-foot wharf and home. This cove became known as Davenport's Landing, later simply referred to as Davenport Landing.

Several businesses were growing up around Davenport Landing. Sawmills dotted the landscape. Swiss and Italian dairy farmers moved into the area and purchased the sprawling rancheros. The very early dairies were owned by the Respini, Moretti, Morelli, and Filippini families, who joined together and incorporated as the Coast Dairies and Land Company in 1901. One of the first goals of the newly formed corporation was to establish a town, and San Vicente by-the-Sea (later Davenport) was born. At the same time, efforts were underway to extract and process limestone in the San Vicente bluffs. But it was the establishment of a massive cement plant in 1905–1906 that transformed Davenport into a "company town." The cement plant created hundreds of jobs and attracted immigrants from many countries. Their diverse backgrounds helped shape and influence life in this rural community. Railroads were built to transport people and goods to and from the area. In 1906, the Davenport Landing Post Office was moved one mile south, and its name came along for the ride. The postal stop at San Vicente by-the-Sea officially became known as Davenport.

As the United States became more entangled in World War I and a possible draft loomed in the future, most of the Swiss dairymen involved with the Coast Dairies and Land Company returned to Switzerland in order to comply with neutrality laws and manage their interests back home. By 1920, most of the shareholders had left California. Remarkably, the Swiss-owned Coast Dairies and Land Company continued to exist and was overseen by local supervisors until it was sold to the Trust for Public Land in 1998.

Over the years, life has changed considerably for residents of the seaside town. The sawmills, dairies, and wharves are no more. The cement plant sleeps on the hillside north of town, abandoned. Tourists swing through town for lunch and to stretch their legs or comb the beach for a few hours before continuing on to their destinations. The tiny town between Santa Cruz and San Francisco enfolds a surprisingly vibrant mixture of citizens. Artisans, restaurateurs, teachers, business owners, students, and retired folks delight in Davenport's charm and unique sense of place.

Travelers along Highway 1 are still able to take in the pristine countryside, redwood and oak forests, rolling meadows, grasslands, and sweeping ocean views, but Davenport was once a complex, bustling, and industrious center full of vibrant tales of its people, whales, lumber, dairies, and limestone.

One

NATIVE PEOPLE AND
EARLY EXPLORERS

OHLONE WINTER CAMP. Indigenous people lived along the California coast for at least 12,000 years. The tribe that resided in the Davenport area were the Cotoni. They made their homes along the marine coastal terraces and into the foothills of the Santa Cruz Mountains. The Cotoni were one of more than 50 tribelets that formed the Ohlone language group. They spoke the Awaswas dialect. (Courtesy of Mark Hylkema.)

OHLONE DEER HUNTER. The Cotoni were skilled hunters, gatherers, and excellent gardeners. They managed the land by implementing principles including the use of fire to clear fields. They hunted a wide variety of animals, such as deer, elk, bears, rabbits, ducks, geese, sea mammals, lizards, snakes, and grasshoppers. Nearby rivers and lagoons provided the Cotoni with salmon, mussels, abalone, kelp, sea salt, and other seafood. (Courtesy of Mark Hylkema.)

OHLONE NECKLACE AND OLIVELLA SHELLS. The shell-rich shores near Davenport provided the native people with valuable resources, such as abalone for pendants and olivella shells that were used to make beads, which were a prized commodity. The shell beads were traded with neighboring tribes and have been found as far east as Nevada. Local chert was also plentiful and used for making knives and arrow tips. (Courtesy of Mark Hylkema.)

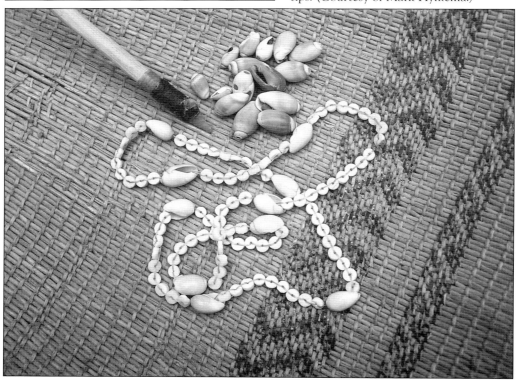

OHLONE GIFT BASKET, 1885. Ohlone women were expert basket makers. Specialized baskets were constructed for storage, gathering food, winnowing seeds, carrying water, and cooking meals. Ornate gift baskets, used to hold an individual's belongings, were embellished with shell beads and colorful feathers. Few early Ohlone baskets have survived and are housed in museums in California; Washington, DC; Paris; and Russia. (Courtesy of Santa Cruz Museum of Natural History.)

SAN SALVADOR REPLICA, 2018. Known as the first European visitor to California, in 1542, Juan Rodriguez Cabrillo laid claim to the coast for Spain. Rumblings that Russia or England might claim parts of California for themselves prompted Spain to act. In 1602, Sebastian Vizcaino sailed along the coast in search of safe harbors for New Spain's trade ships, eventually making his way to and naming Monterey Bay. This photograph is of the *San Salvador*, an exact replica of Cabrillo's flagship built by the Maritime Museum of San Diego. (Photograph by Jerry Soto.)

PORTOLÁ VISITS THE NORTH COAST. In 1769, Capt. Gaspar de Portolá and Padre Juan Crespi led the campaign to explore Alta California by land and to establish Spanish settlements along the way. This journey resulted in the formation of two missions, one in San Diego and the other in Carmel, as well as presidios in both San Diego and Monterey. In search of Vizcaino's Monterey Bay, which they saw but did not recognize, the Portolá expedition pushed farther north and discovered San Francisco Bay. According to California state archeologist Mark Hylkema, "The Portolá expedition definitely traveled through Cotoni country in the fall of 1769. They had 200 horses and mules, and about sixty-six members." According to expedition diaries, the group camped near Majors Creek just south of Davenport on October 18, 1769, and the following night on a hill above the confluence of Scott Creek and Molino Creek, a few miles to the north. The approximate location is shown here. (Photograph by Ed Dickie.)

SANTA CRUZ MISSION, EARLY 1900S POSTCARD. The Cotoni were the last of the local indigenous people brought to Mission Santa Cruz, which was founded in 1791. Lorenzo Asisara was the last local native person to reside here. It is believed that he was descended from the Cotoni. He gave three interviews in his later years, recalling a harsh life within the mission walls. (Courtesy of Frank Perry.)

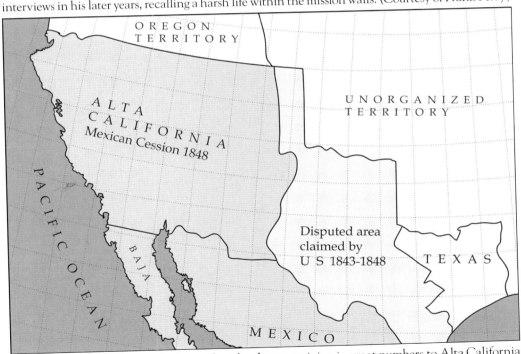

MAP OF ALTA CALIFORNIA. Traders and settlers began arriving in great numbers to Alta California from the United States and Europe in the 1830s. The United States' efforts to expand across the entire continent of North America resulted in the Mexican-American War, which raged from April 1846 to February 1848. The United States acquired 500,000 square miles of Mexican territory under the Treaty of Guadalupe Hidalgo. (Courtesy of Sage Lee.)

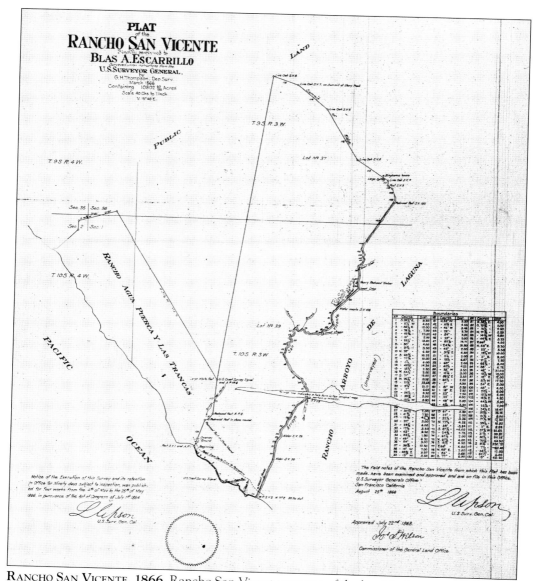

RANCHO SAN VICENTE, 1866. Rancho San Vicente was one of the last Mexican grants given out by Gov. Pio Pico before the 1848 Treaty of Guadalupe Hidalgo. As required by the Land Act of 1851, a claim for Rancho San Vicente was filed, and the grant was successfully patented to Blas A. Escarrillo. In 1865, Escarrillo sold Rancho San Vicente to Josiah, Charles, and Asa Stanford, marking the end of Mexican land ownership on the North Coast. Excluding Davenport Landing, which is partially in the Agua Puerca rancho, the town of Davenport sits within the boundaries of Rancho San Vicente. The San Vicente creek watershed held the bulk of natural resources that fueled the early industries. The creek itself was the primary natural boundary separating Rancho San Vicente from Rancho Arroyo de la Laguna and is shown here at right center.

Two

PIONEERS, DAIRYMEN, WHALES, AND LANDINGS

JAMES WILLIAMS WITH SONS ISAAC AND JONATHAN, 1850s. James Williams and his brother Squire purchased the Rancho Arroyo de la Laguna land grant in 1847. On Arroyo de los Lobos, he established Williams Landing, the first ship landing in the area. The Williams brothers also built a house and sawmill nearby. Williams Landing was used to transport lumber, lime, and produce along the central coast and to San Francisco. (Courtesy of the Williams family.)

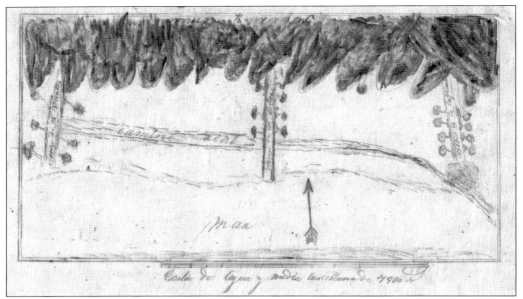

MAP OF RANCHO ARROYO DE LA LAGUNA, C. 1840S. This document shows a highly simplified map of the 4,418-acre rancho the Williams brothers purchased. On the left is San Vicente Creek, on the right is Laguna Creek, and at center is Arroyo de los Lobos (named for seals barking at the coast) or in modern times, Liddell Creek. Note the mountains and tree symbols along the creek. Most of this property was eventually acquired by Jeremiah Respini and became a significant part of the Coast Dairies property. (Courtesy of UC Berkeley, Bancroft Library.)

DINGWALL'S BARK CAMP, 1860. Local Californian tanoak bark was stripped from trees and loaded onto wagons bound for tanneries in and around Santa Cruz. The tannin-rich bark was dried for several months before the tanning process could begin. Rustic cabins, pictured here, were single-wall units constructed without foundations, which made them easier to relocate as lumbering activities advanced across the region. (Courtesy of Patty Morelli.)

BOSTON TANNERY, 1866. There were five tanneries within Santa Cruz city limits in the 1860s. Pictured is a large tannery owned by Joseph B. and Eliza Boston just below High Street, overlooking the city. Over by the San Lorenzo River was the Kron tannery, which in later years under the leadership of Ansley Kullman Salz became the Salz tannery. The Salz tannery was well known for its California saddle leather. (Courtesy of the Library of Congress.)

CHINA LADDER, LATE 1800s. Chinese divers frequently harvested abalone off the coastal terrace near Scott's Creek. According to *Historic Spots in California* by Mildred Brooke Hoover, "On the bluff was a shack in which several Chinese men lived. They harvested abalone from the rocks below and dried them for the Chinese trade. From the bluff, they followed a trail, down a rope, and finally a ladder to reach the beach."

CAPT. JOHN DAVENPORT. John Pope Davenport was born in Tiverton, Rhode Island, in 1818 and went to sea at age 12. According to *Ship Registers of New Bedford, Massachusetts, of 1852*, Davenport was master of the *Alfred*, a 180-ton whaling schooner that worked the waters of the South Pacific. During off-seasons, he imported goods such as fresh fruits and vegetables to new towns and settlements along the California coast from Monterey Bay to San Francisco. On one trip, Captain Davenport observed numerous humpback whales not far from shore. The whales were surfacing every two minutes, and they seemed unafraid of his approaching ship. He concluded these whales could be easily captured and envisioned a new and prosperous life for himself in California. Davenport returned to New Bedford and sold his interest in the *Alfred*. (Courtesy of MAH.)

ELLEN CLARK SMITH. In 1852, John Davenport married his second cousin Ellen Clark Smith in Fairhaven, Massachusetts. He was 34, and she was 18 years old. The newlyweds set out for California. According to Ellen's diary, their ship was disabled along the Caribbean coast, and passengers were forced to walk or ride mules 200 miles across Nicaragua. She also noted that they contracted "Panama Fever" along the way. (Courtesy of MAH.)

SAN JUAN DEL SUR, NICARAGUA, 2010. The group left San Juan del Sur aboard the *Pioneer*, but had to evacuate due to damage acquired earlier, near Cape Horn. The *Sea Bird* transported them to San Francisco. Captain Davenport leased the *Otranto*, and as they entered Monterey Bay, Ellen exclaimed, "Everyone is entitled to one glimpse of the Promised Land, and this is it." (Photograph by Leah Davis.)

MONTEREY WHALING STATION, 1850S. John Pope Davenport established the first shore whaling station in Monterey in 1854. He hired a Portuguese whaling crew who resided in the white adobe house shown here. John and Ellen lived in the first red-clay brick building in California, at left. During off-seasons, Captain Davenport leased the *Caroline Foote* and sailed to Baja California in search of whales. (Courtesy of Monterey Public Library.)

OLD FASHIONED DARK GINGERBREAD

1 cup dark molasses
½ cup Crisco shortening
1 cup dairy sour cream
2 cups, 2 T all purpose flour
1 teaspoon baking soda
1 teaspoon each ground ginger, cinnamon
¼ teaspoon ground cloves

Preheat oven to 350 degrees. Line a 9x13 baking pan with parchment paper and lightly grease with oil or butter. Sift flour, soda, and spices together and set aside. Bring molasses and shortening to a full boil in a pan large enough to hold entire recipe. Cool molasses mixture a few minutes and whisk in the sour cream and then the flour mixture. Spread evenly in the prepared pan and bake for 30 to 40 minutes or until a tester tests clean. Cool 5 minutes in the pan and then turn out onto a wire rack to complete cooling. Cut into serving size pieces.

As served at the Cooper Molera Adobe for
Christmas in the Adobes
Monterey State Historic Park
Monterey, California

GINGERBREAD RECIPE. This recipe was most certainly one that Ellen Davenport would have used in her Monterey kitchen. There were few recipes in circulation. Local ladies gathered at church or social functions and shared favorite recipes with one another. Lard or butter would have been used instead of shortening in earlier versions. (Courtesy of Traci Bliss and the Monterey State Historic Park.)

THE WHALER. David Bertão explains in *The Portuguese Shore Whalers of California 1854–1904*, "California shore whaling in the nineteenth century was a brutal and frightening way to make a living. Its reliance on small boats and primitive guns put the shore whalers' lives at risk every time they attempted a capture." (Photograph by Manuel Dias; CSU Stanislaus Library, PHPC, 2006.)

ARCHIBALD CHEESE HOUSE, 2003. James Archibald, from Scotland, was one of the first dairymen in the area. In 1867, he purchased the Rancho Agua Puerca y las Trancas land grant from Ramon Rodriguez and Francisco Alviso. Ambriogio Gianone, who worked for Archibald, built this earthen cheese house specifically to produce Swiss cheese. Archibald died in 1875 while in Scotland, and the rancho was sold to dairyman Joseph Bloom. (Photograph by Ed Dickie.)

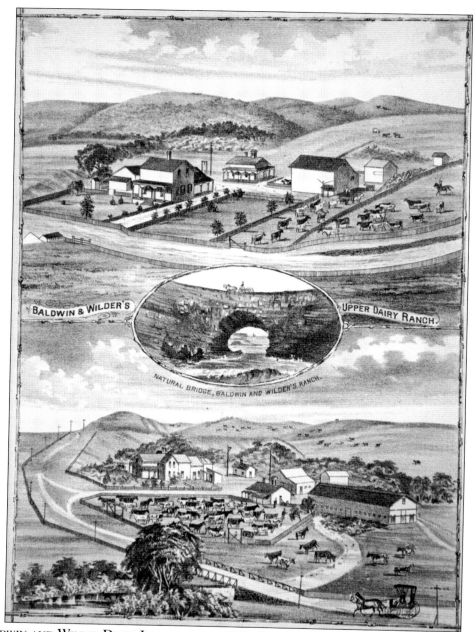

Labels within illustration:
BALDWIN & WILDER'S — UPPER DAIRY RANCH.
NATURAL BRIDGE, BALDWIN AND WILDER'S RANCH.

BALDWIN AND WILDER DAIRY ILLUSTRATION, 1879. By 1850, most of the North Coast Mexican landowners had sold their properties to new settlers, many of whom were Swiss Italians with experience in dairy operations. Starting at the Baldwin (later purchased by Joseph Scaroni) and Wilder dairies, there were the Leonard Tenbrook Almstead dairy, which became the Pio Scaroni dairy; the Eagle Glen Dairy, run by Antone Sylva from the Azores islands; the Horace Gushee ranch, which became a dairy owned by Joseph Enright and later Tom Majors (Laguna ranch); the Yellow Bank dairy, and a short distance up the road, the Mocettini Dairy. Further on were the Tiarone (owned by Adam Gilchrist), Chandler, Filippini, Gianone, and Steele dairies, among others. (Courtesy of Santa Cruz Public Library.)

MOCETTINI DAIRY. The Mocettini Dairy was just north of Davenport. Antonio Mocettini, a native of Switzerland, worked for 52 years as a dairyman, making him one of the last dairymen on the Coast Road. G.P. Laird was the previous owner. Mocettini specialized in a type of Monterey jack cheese. He was a member of the Santa Cruz Grove of Druids. His wife, Vangie, was a well-known nurse in the area. (Courtesy of Patty Morelli.)

YELLOWBANK DAIRY BEING RAZED, 1955. In the 1880s, Jeremiah Respini started a small dairy on this property, which over time grew into a significant operation. He and neighbor Louis Moretti became business partners in 1901 when they formed the Coast Dairies and Land Company. The dairy sat near the mouth of what was once Respini Creek, today's Yellow Bank Creek. The Ocean Shore Railway had a small flag-stop there and transported both beach-seeking tourists and local dairy products. (Courtesy of Ruth-Marion Baruch and Pirkle Jones Photographs and Papers. Special Collections and Archives, University Library, University of California, Santa Cruz.)

CHANDLER DAIRY, EARLY 1900s. The Lewis Chandler Dairy owned 136 acres and about 100 head of cattle just north of Davenport on land now owned by the Molino Creek Farm Collective. The Chandler dairy sat further inland from the coast, where summers were warmer and the road to market longer. (Courtesy of Patty Morelli.)

THE GYPSY. Built in 1888, the steam schooner *Gypsy* was active in the Monterey Bay and called in Santa Cruz three times a week from San Francisco. It was used by dairy farmers to ship products, including cheese, milk, butter, and creams. At its peak, the Scaroni dairy produced 300 pounds of cheese per day, most of which was transported by the *Gypsy* until it ran aground near Monterey in 1905. The railroad soon arrived and took over the transport of most North Coast products. (Courtesy of MAH.)

BITUMEN MINING, 1860s. Black asphaltum, also known as bitumen, was discovered in the upper canyon near Majors Creek. Dairymen Joe Enright and Pio Scaroni owned much of the bitumen-producing land in the area. Over the years, several attempts were made to extract oil from the region, but ultimately, the deposit was mostly used for making paving material. Local entrepreneur Fred Swanton also got involved and helped create the Santa Cruz Oil Company.

N. P. INGALLS.   ANDREW T. TA

SAN MATEO AND SANTA CRUZ

STAGE LINE,

TAFT & INGALLS, PROPRIETORS.

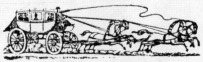

These Stages leave Pescadero at 8 A. M., arriving in Santa Cruz at 4 P. M.; Leaving Santa Cruz at 8 A. M., on the day following, they reach Pescadero at 4 P M.

From Pescadero, the places passed *"en route"* are, Pigeon Point, Point New Years, Sea Side, Laurel Grove, Berry's Falls, Davenport's Landing, Williams' Landing and Hall's Natural Bridge.

At many parts of the road the Scenery is noticeably fine, the Roads are excellent, and in the well-appointed "Conveyances" of this Company, and behind their Spirited Horses, the ride is exhilarating and pleasant. This trip cannot but prove satisfactory to anyone undertaking it.

STAGE LINE ADVERTISEMENT. In the late 1860s, residents along the coast depended upon the stagecoach to transport their products to market. In good weather and when tides were low, it took about nine hours to travel from Santa Cruz to San Mateo. In winter, when roads were rain-soaked and cliffs unstable, the journey was often delayed by several hours or days. (Courtesy of Lud McCrary.)

JENNIE THELIN AND CREW. The lumber schooner *Jennie Thelin* was built at Davenport's Landing in 1869. In 1904, the *Jennie Thelin* was registered in San Francisco under the Mexican flag by E.F. Scott and given a new name, *Carmencita*. The ship disappeared for three months and was discovered poaching seals off the coast of Siberia. Several well-armed Russians along the coast spotted the ship and one of its small boats carrying three sailors and opened fire from the shore. Only 200 yards out, the little boat was an easy target. It was reported that one of the sailors in the boat had six of his lower teeth shattered by gunfire. The *Carmencita* then made speed for Dutch Harbor, Alaska. When this news reached US and Mexican authorities, all connections to the vessel were quickly denied, and the *Carmencita*'s registration papers were canceled on the spot. (Both, courtesy of San Francisco Maritime National Historical Park.)

DAVENPORT LANDING WHARVES. In 1869, John Davenport rented one acre of land at the mouth of Agua Puerca (Muddy Waters) Creek, built a family home and, at the request of local dairy and lumbermen, a 450-foot wharf. Whaling gear and blubber-melting try pots were also brought in. The cove became known as Davenport's Landing. The wharf was an immediate success but required constant repairs due to wave damage. (Courtesy of Sage Lee.)

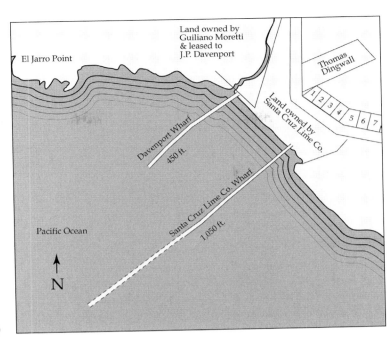

DAVENPORT LANDING BEACH, PRE-1913. John Davenport's arrival in 1869 brought not only a wharf, but also accompanying business. By 1875, the village, referred to as Davenport's Landing, had two hotels, two general stores, saloons, a blacksmith shop, a butcher shop, a livery stable, and shipyard. The busy landing also attracted a summer holiday crowd, such as the children pictured here with Davenport Landing in the background.

THOMAS DINGWALL AND CO., 1872. This general store ad is from Paulson's business directory. Paulson's once called Davenport Landing the best roadstead in the county, outside of Santa Cruz city. A wide variety of ocean fish were easily harvested along Davenport Landing, including the newly popular delicacy of the time: abalone. (Courtesy of Lud McCrary.)

UTT'S HOTEL ADVERTISEMENT, 1872. Lewis A. Utt, proprietor of one of the hotels in Davenport Landing, promised sandy beaches, beautiful ocean views, and comfortable, resort-like accommodations for tourists and hunters alike. There was also a stable on the premises to care for the guests' horses. (Courtesy of Lud McCrary.)

AGUA PUERCA SCHOOLHOUSE, 2005. Agua Puerca schoolhouse was originally located near Scott Creek, despite the fact that most students lived at Davenport Landing. Locals enjoy telling of a night in 1908 when several men moved the building four miles south to Davenport Landing. The community was shocked to find the schoolhouse magically relocated the following morning. Agua Puerca school closed in 1940. (Courtesy of Ginaia Kelly.)

DAVENPORT LANDING RESIDENCE, 2004. Built around 1908 and dismantled in 2008, this house was one of very few that survived the fire of 1913. Owners in modern times included Priscilla Noyce, niece of Intel cofounder Robert Noyce. As of 2019, Moore's Law namesake Gordon Moore, also an Intel co-founder, owns a beachfront home at Davenport Landing. (Courtesy of Ginaia Kelly.)

JOHN EDWARD AND HARROLD "OLLIE" DAVENPORT AND THE SS DAVENPORT, C. 1913. Two of John Davenport's sons, John Jr. and Harrold "Ollie," started the Davenport Steamship Lines out of San Francisco. The company built three steamships that transported lumber, dairy, and other products along the West Coast as far north as Puget Sound. Perhaps to honor their father, or as a nod to their childhood home of Davenport Landing, the brothers christened one of their steamships the SS *Davenport*. Other ships built by the Davenport Steamship Lines were the SS *Fairhaven* and MS *Monterey*. The company also had one sailing vessel in their fleet. (Both, courtesy of Bill Lewis.)

Three

LUMBER, LIME, AND BIG CEMENT

OXEN TEAM, 1890s. Early lumber crews used oxen teams similar to these to pull downed trees out from the woods through steep ravines and to nearby sawmills. Oxen were slow and steady helpers, capable of pulling very heavy loads for long periods of time. The lead oxen followed signals and voice commands barked out by the ox-driver.

TWO-SPOOL DONKEY ENGINE, EARLY 1900S. In 1881, John Dolbeer from Eureka, California, invented a steam-powered winch that greatly improved local logging and mining operations in the San Vicente area. Steam "donkeys" also powered cranes and hoists and provided power to the pulley system used to transport lumber and other materials between Davenport Landing and ships anchored near the shore. The town's public baths can be seen just up the street.

SAN VICENTE LUMBER COMPANY, EARLY 1900S. The San Vicente Lumber Company was formed in 1909 when William Dingee sold the timber rights to a group of lumbermen from Salt Lake City. The Ocean Shore Railway transported logs from the Davenport area to the west side of Santa Cruz, where the company created a millpond by damming Moore's Creek (today's Antonelli's Pond). Since the company was run by Mormons, the workers were required to donate 10 percent of their wages to the church.

SAN VICENTE LUMBER COMPANY RAILROAD. Here is a stretch of the San Vicente Lumber Company right-of-way with a steam donkey at left. Over nine miles of broad-gauge railroad were built, with grades reaching eight percent. From 1908 to 1923, over 600 million board feet of redwood lumber was harvested in the various watersheds in the hills behind Davenport, including upper San Vicente Creek. (Courtesy Mattei Family Collection, MAH.)

BIG CREEK WATER COMPANY, 1896. Fred Swanton of Santa Cruz, who was active in promoting all things Santa Cruz, brought electricity to the town by building the third hydroelectric power station in California. It was located on Big Creek in the hills north of Davenport. During the drought years of 1897–1899, water flow was limited, and steam generators fueled by redwood trees from the surrounding hills were purchased to provide more reliable power. (Courtesy of Lud McCrary.)

GUSTAVE REIS. In 1873, brothers Gustave, Christian, and Ferdinand Reis, interested in developing the lime deposits near the San Vicente Creek, purchased 8,145 acres of the Rancho San Vicente land grant and incorporated as the Santa Cruz Lime Company. They negotiated the use of John Davenport's wharf and loaned him $2,900 for repairs. When Davenport's wharf became unusable for a period, they built their own wharf parallel to it. The Reis brothers built a ship, the *San Vicente*, to transport lime along the California coast.

THE WHARF WARS, SANTA CRUZ COURT HOUSE, 1867. In 1876, John Davenport claimed that ships could no longer dock at his wharf due to the proximity of the Santa Cruz Lime Company's wharf. The ruling favored Davenport, which infuriated Gustave Reis, who called in Davenport's loan. By 1878, both wharves were standing idle. At age 60 Davenport moved to Santa Cruz, where he worked in real estate and served as a justice of the peace. In 1892, he died in San Francisco at 73. Ellen Davenport died in 1922 at 87. (Courtesy of MAH.)

THE NEW SANTA CRUZ LIME COMPANY, 1905. Disappointed with the court's wharf ruling and under the shadow of increased taxes, Gustave Reis and partners began to lose interest in their lime company. In 1896, company president Robert Ewing threatened to sell the company if taxes were increased. The assessor held firm, and the company was sold to Frederick W. Billing (pictured) and John Q. Packard. (Courtesy of MAH.)

SAN VICENTE CREEK LIME KILNS AND QUARRY, C. 1905. The Santa Cruz Lime Company successfully produced lime at the San Vicente creek location from 1875 to 1876 and later with the new owners from 1901 to 1906. With builders moving toward using the stronger and more waterproof Portland cement instead of lime, these lumber-fueled lime kilns would soon go cold.

WILLIAM J. DINGEE, "THE CEMENT KING," 1903. William Jackson Dingee became a millionaire by way of savvy real estate investments and his Oakland Water Company. By the end of World War I, Dingee had a San Francisco mansion, lushly referred to as "Diamond Place," and two million-dollar mansions on New York's fashionable Fifth Avenue. "The Cement King" had been investigating area lime-rock deposits, and in 1903, plans were in the works to build a large cement plant on Escalona Drive in Santa Cruz. Dingee's ambitious plan was met with fierce resistance from members of the community. After months of public outcry, he withdrew the offer. Determined to organize a plant nearby, he set his sights on San Vicente by-the-Sea, 10 miles to the north. The Cement King was preparing to build one of the largest cement plants the United States would ever know. (Courtesy of Oakland Public Library.)

ARTIST'S CONCEPTION OF CEMENT PLANT, 1905. In April 1905, William Dingee and his partner Irving Bachman purchased the Santa Cruz Lime Company property and secured 95 acres from the Coast Dairies and Land Company. Bay Counties Electric brought in electricity. Southern Pacific sent surveyors. The Al Cox sawmill on San Vicente Creek began cutting timber, and ships anchored offshore, loaded with construction materials bound for the new cement plant.

"THE CHUTES," DAVENPORT BEACH, 1905. With no railroad yet, the new Santa Cruz Lime Company devised an overhead cable system that loaded barrels of lime onto waiting ships just off the beach. Although not as desirable as a sheltered harbor, this system did succeed in moving lime to market if no storms were threatening. Anchors and land tie-downs were utilized to keep the ships as stationary as possible. The same system was also used to load materials for the construction of the cement plant.

116.- Healy & Tibbitts Cons. Co's. Camp - Jan. 1, 1906.

HEALY AND TIBBITTS LABOR CAMP. There was plenty of manpower in the early 1900s. The cement plant's labor contractor, Healy and Tibbitts, formed a bustling tent city for new recruits, many of whom had recently immigrated to the United States. In 1907, quarry workers received about $2 per day, with incentives for quick work. It was considered a good wage at the time.

S.C.P.C. Co. Train on Trestle No. 1. Jan. 10, 1907.

QUARRY CRUSHER BRIDGE, 1908. The limestone quarry, known either as Bella Vista or San Vicente, and nearby shale quarry provided raw materials used to make the Portland cement produced by the new Santa Cruz Portland Cement Company. An enormous rock crusher was installed next to the quarry to process the materials before they were transported by steam locomotives down the San Vicente Creek canyon to the main plant.

QUARRY TRAIN, 1907. The nearly four-mile rail line between the limestone quarry and the cement plant involved seven trestle bridges that were not entirely stable. By 1916, most of these trestles were filled in. This dramatic photograph shows what was probably the last bridge ravine crossing on the way back to the plant. Despite the close proximity, this railroad never connected with the Ocean Shore Railway or Coast Line Railroad.

MOVING THE TRACKS, 1907. Intense and exhausting manual labor was required in the early years at the quarry. As limestone was removed from the face of the hillside, moveable tracks, installed by hand, were necessary to bring rail cars closer to the exposed rock. Quarry work was dangerous, and on occasion, serious and even deadly accidents occurred. Steam donkeys can be seen in this photograph, working tirelessly in the background.

MINING BEACH SAND, 1907. A sand hoist skip was used to mine the sand from the beach below. This work was dependent on the schedules of the ocean tides. This raw material was added in small amounts to the processed limestone and shale when making cement. Note the absence of the large cypress tree grove seen today.

KILN EXTENSION, 1908. The cement plant was a constant work in progress. As demand for cement increased, so did capacity. This photograph shows the construction of the final 12 rotary kilns, bringing the total to 24. By 1908, the plant was producing upwards of 10,000 barrels of cement a day, with most of it going to post-earthquake rebuilding in San Francisco and Oakland.

DAVENPORT TRAIN DEPOT, 1910. Pictured here are farmers shipping produce from the Davenport Depot, built by the Coast Line Railroad. The railroads dramatically reduced the time it took to transport fresh produce and dairy products from farm to market. Keeping produce fresh over longer distances became a reality with the introduction of refrigerated train cars. Soon, national and international markets opened up for Davenport's niche products like Brussels sprouts and artichokes.

STILL LOOKING FOR DINGEE, 1908. Newspapers across California documented the rise and fall of William J. Dingee. Apparent mismanagement of funds sent Dingee into a tailspin. He transferred his mansions into his wife's name and fled to France. Upon his return to California, Dingee faced his debts and, in 1921, declared bankruptcy. In 1941, he died in obscurity; his last known occupation was listed as a night watchman.

STILL LOOKING FOR DINGEE

SAN FRANCISCO, Dec. 3.—Acting upon the assumption that William J. Dingee will be disqualified, Attorney Frank C. Drew is seeking other persons to go on the bond of Eugene E. Schmitz.

The investigation into Dingee's financial ability to meet the bond came up before udge Dunne yesterday, but on the showing that Dingee had not been served, was continued one week.

The officers have not been able to find Dingee in order to serve him, while Schmitz has not been able thus far to get another bondsman.

BERTHA BILLING COOPE, C. 1880S. In 1906, John Packard and other board members sold their shares of the Santa Cruz Lime Company, while Frederick Billing retained his 25 percent interest. After Billing's death in 1914, his interest was passed on to his daughter, Bertha (Billing) Coope. She served as an active board member of the Santa Cruz Lime Company well into her 90s. It was said that when plant personnel received word that Bertha was coming in, they quickly cleaned up the office, which included removing any "girly" pictures from the walls. Bertha died in 1956 at age 105. (Courtesy of MAH.)

Four

A Town Is Born

EARLY DAVENPORT, 1908. In 1907, the post office at Davenport Landing was moved to the much larger village of San Vicente by-the-Sea, a mile to the south. The post office retained the name Davenport, and gradually, the name San Vicente faded away. Davenport provided residents with a schoolhouse, church, hospital, hotels, restaurants, blacksmith shop, bakery, butcher shop, and saloons. (Photograph by Ole Ravnos.)

OLD COAST ROAD, POST-1915. The town now known as Davenport was built and managed by Coast Dairies and Land Company. The day-long journey to Santa Cruz was a hot and dusty ride in the summer and a very muddy one during the winter. The old Coast Road on the right remained a narrow dirt road up until the late 1930s. With the arrival of the cement plant, Davenport reached its maximum population of around 800 in the early 1900s.

SAN VICENTE CREEK RAMPART, 1906. To transport heavy cement, North Coast train trestles were filled in by trains dumping earth from a temporary trestle. The old creek bed can be seen being buried in the foreground, forever reducing the wetlands of San Vicente to a channelized creek. Looking closer, the cement plant, Old Town, and on the point, the shipping derrick and lime storage building, are visible. It is likely that the redwood trestles have at least partially survived inside the ramparts. (Courtesy of Covello and Covello.)

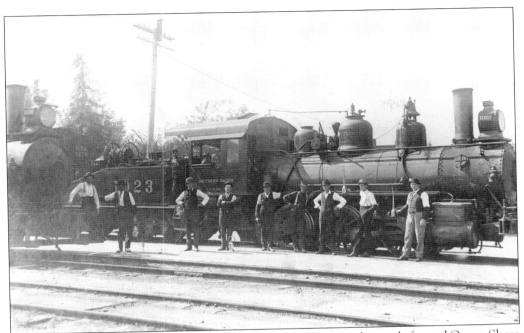

SOUTHERN PACIFIC RAILROAD COMPANY. With competition from the newly formed Ocean Shore Railway, the race was on to complete a route between San Francisco and Santa Cruz. Southern Pacific created the subsidiary Coast Line Railroad just for this route in 1905. With good business coming from the cement plant and resources stretched from the 1906 earthquake, Coast Line stopped construction at Davenport. In 1917, after being merged back into its parent company, Southern Pacific would soon be the sole coast-side railroad, serving the North Coast until 1996.

OCEAN SHORE RAILWAY COMPANY. With the initial goal of building a double-tracked, standard-gauge, electric railroad line 80 miles in length, Ocean Shore laid out routes from Santa Cruz to beyond San Vicente. Although Ocean Shore failed to complete the line, north and south segments did get used. In the south, revenue was mostly from transporting lumber, but passenger service was offered. Finances never recovered after the 1906 earthquake, and the Ocean Shore Railroad ceased operations in 1920.

FIRST RAILS ARRIVE, 1906. By January 1906, Ocean Shore Railway had completed the line from Santa Cruz to Davenport. In roughly four months, 10 large trestles and 12 miles of track were constructed. Regular service began in mid-1906, but it was not long before Coast Line Railroad began service. The barn at center, which was still standing in 2019, was used for building containers for agricultural products and storage.

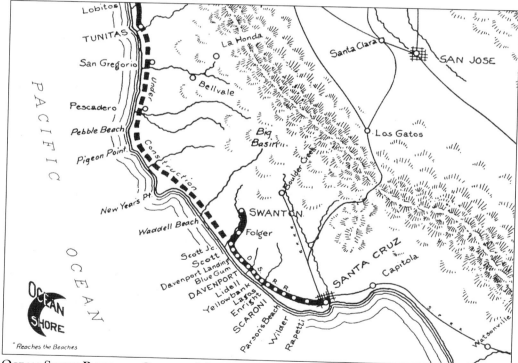

OCEAN SHORE RAILROAD COMPANY MAP, 1913. This excerpt from a publicity folder shows the southern end of the route and popular stops. Most were dairies. The price was 50¢ for a trip from Santa Cruz to San Vicente. Starting in 1914, Ocean Shore operated a Stanley Steamer autobus between Swanton and Tunitas (dashed line). Other Ocean Shore ventures included a proposed resort town named Folger, after the investor and coffee magnate. (Courtesy of Ted Wurm.)

COMPANY TOWN, 1909. The meat market and town baths can be seen next to the Cash Store. With the exception of the small worker cabins closer to the cement plant, every structure in this photograph used as a residence is still standing. The large towers in the distance were primarily used to move "klinker," a semi-finished product, from the kiln to the storage shed before the finishing process. (Photograph by Ole Ravnos.)

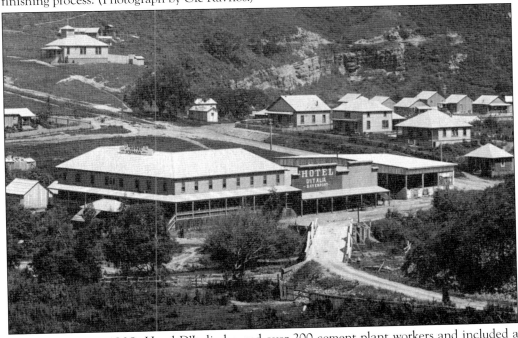

HOTEL D'ITALIA, 1908. Hotel D'Italia housed over 200 cement plant workers and included a restaurant and adjoining horse stable. The hotel provided a sense of community for early Italian immigrants. Originally built by the Coast Dairies and Land Company, it was sold to Josephine Micossi and the Frank Bragazzi estate in 1923. The hotel was destroyed by fire in 1945. (Photograph by Ole Ravnos.)

NEWLY BUILT OCEAN VIEW HOTEL, 1906.
The Coast Dairies and Land Company built this hotel on the main coast road primarily to house employees of the cement plant. It was built out of redwood milled at the San Vicente lumber mill and hauled down by horse-drawn wagons. The cement for the foundation came from Napa Junction, one of William Dingee's other cement plants, since the Davenport cement plan was not in operation yet.

CHARLIE BELLA, 1950s. For Charlie Bella, an Italian immigrant, the American dream became a reality when he and his brother John purchased the Ocean View Hotel in 1919. Charlie's daughter recalls, "Dad worked for the San Vicente Logging Mill. He said that he never dreamed that when he was helping to fall those logs that they would go for the hotel that he would someday own." Charlie Bella's wife, Carmela, attracted many customers with her famous spaghetti dinners.

DORELLO MORELLI AND FAMILY, 1914. Dorello Morelli immigrated to San Diego at age 15. He worked on dairy ranches in Monterey County, later making his way to Yellow Bank Dairy near Davenport. He was an active member of the Coast Dairy and Land Company and later became vice president. Morelli ran the Davenport Cash Store for 49 years and also served as postmaster for two decades.

DAVENPORT CASH STORE, c. 1908. The Davenport Cash Store stocked just about everything, including groceries, household goods, clothing, fishing tackle, hunting gear, farm machinery parts, tires, animal feed, and liquor. Quarry workers cashed their paychecks here before heading down the street to the local restaurants and saloons. Dorello Morelli was known to be a charitable and honest shopkeeper. He offered free deliveries and often extended credit to local farmers.

NEW TOWN OF MORETTIVILLE, 1910. With a workers' strike in full swing, four blocks of houses were built just north of the plant for foremen and superintendents in an attempt to separate the workers from supervisors and maintain production. Originally called Morettiville after Louis Moretti of the Coast Dairies and Land Company, locals have always referred to it as New Town. This area of Davenport was normally upwind from the plant's dust plume.

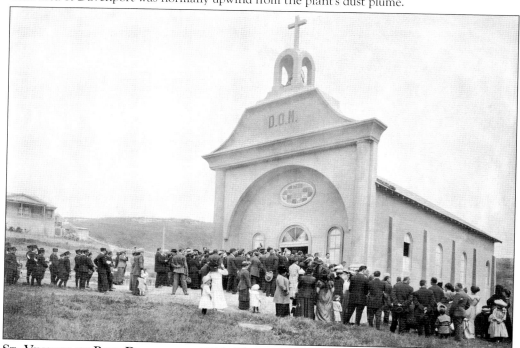

ST. VINCENT DE PAUL DEDICATION, 1915. The town's Catholic church was built in 1914–1915 with materials and labor donated by the Coast Dairies and Land Company, cement plant, and residents. The church was designed by Louis Moretti after similar churches in Switzerland. The Holy Cross choir and a high school band from Santa Cruz entertained crowds at the church's dedication on May 16, 1915. Louis Moretti and his family emigrated back to Switzerland shortly after this dedication, along with many of the other Swiss Coast Dairies and Land Company leaders.

PACIFIC SCHOOLHOUSE. The *Santa Cruz Sentinel* of January 25, 1908, reported there were 83 children enrolled in the Pacific School District who hailed from 22 states and the countries of Switzerland, Spain, Italy, France, Germany, Greece, Norway, and Sweden. Notice the filled-in railroad trestle at far right, and the old coastal road in the background at left, with a horse and buggy heading toward Santa Cruz. Below is another view of the Pacific Schoolhouse, with the newly built Catholic church just next door. Teacher Mr. Levy, shown here with students, was the schoolmaster from 1912 to 1918. A wood-burning potbellied stove near the entrance kept the building warm during the winter months. The school also offered night classes for adults who were new to the country and in need of English language courses.

QUARRY WORKERS. In the fall of 1905, help-wanted ads appeared in area newspapers, and labor contractors for the cement plant were sent to San Francisco to enlist job-hungry immigrants. The work was back-breaking and the days were long, but quarry work provided a steady income for young men eager to begin their lives in America.

BELLA VISTA, 1920s. Built by the Standard Portland Cement Plant, Bella Vista was a small hamlet near the limestone quarry for the quarry workers and their families. The Italian name was inspired by the beauty of the mountains. A typical Bella Vista duplex home consisted of four rooms with a bath. The town had electricity and running water, but no telephone service. Bella Vista housewives had to be prepared for unannounced visitors at all times.

BELLA VISTA HOTEL/DORMITORIES, 1920s. Single quarry workers stayed in bunkrooms at the Bella Vista Hotel. The complex had a well-regarded kitchen and dining hall large enough to accommodate the hungry men after a grueling day's work at the mine. Despite the town's Italian name, the majority of early quarry workers were from the isle of Crete in Greece.

NARROW-GAUGE ELECTRIC TRAIN, BELLA VISTA, 1920s. An electric engine pulls a line of limestone cars from the mine to the cement plant, passing directly through Bella Vista. The conductor and crew took great pride in the little quarry train. The locomotive was brightly painted with orange and yellow stripes and was polished from coupling-to-whistle. Sometimes, as the train rumbled slowly through the village, the crew would throw a few pieces of candy to waving children.

OPEN-AIR TRANSPORTATION FROM SANTA CRUZ TO PESCADERO, 1914. The Harvey Stage Lines, shown here with drivers Jim Harvey and George McGory, operated daily between San Mateo and Santa Cruz. They were responsible for delivering both passengers and mail to neighboring towns. According to Davenport's Resource Center, it was not uncommon for passengers to have to get out and push a stuck vehicle, and inclement weather was always a possibility.

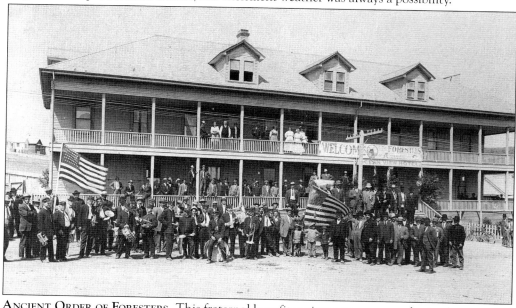

ANCIENT ORDER OF FORESTERS. This fraternal benefit society was very popular in the area, and members often gathered for events in town. Ceremonies with initiations, speeches, food, and dances took place at one of the two large hotels until Foresters Hall was completed in 1913.

DAVENPORT FORESTERS OF AMERICA, 1920S. Seen here is a gathering of the local Foresters of America, Davenport Lodge. The Foresters were a "friendly society" who helped change the insurance industry in favor of working families. They also provided benefits to members and families in need. Among those pictured are Aquilino Ettore Morelli, standing at left holding his hat, and a young Charlie Bella, at top center leaning against the tree.

AQUILINO ETTORE MORELLI, 1920S. Born in Switzerland in 1868, Aquilino Morelli emigrated to California at age 15. In 1906, he joined Coast Dairies and Land Company, eventually becoming the secretary. He established the Forester's Hall, was a member of the Santa Cruz Chamber of Commerce, and vice president of Ocean Shore Canning Company in Half Moon Bay. He also introduced the wildly successful artichoke crops to the area. (Courtesy of Patty Morelli.)

DAVENPORT JAIL, 1914. With the population on the rise, the need for law and order was also on the minds of Davenport residents. When there was an incident, it often took hours for the sheriff from Santa Cruz to arrive on the scene. In the winter, the coastal roads were often impassable. Sheriff Trafton persuaded the Santa Cruz Board of Supervisors to build a jail in Davenport to hold prisoners until one of his deputies was able to pick them up.

DAVENPORT JAIL. Only three legal prisoners were ever registered: a local drunk and two boys from San Mateo county picked up for stealing their uncle's horse. Other jail "guests" were left to release themselves when they had slept off the effects of their evening festivities and were able to walk home unaided. The Ocean View Hotel, with its fine Italian cuisine next door, would serve first-class meals to prisoners at the jail.

Five

THE CULTURAL LIFE

GREEK AND ITALIAN RESIDENTS, 1913. Greek and Italian American residents and guests pose during one of the many community picnics hosted by the Bella Vista Hotel. These gatherings helped local families preserve their cultural heritage through food, music, folk dancing, and storytelling. (Photograph by Ole Ravnos.)

THE GET TOGETHER ORCHESTRA. The Get Together Orchestra was one of the most popular bands in Davenport. They played at many of the picnics, celebrations, and dances in the 1920s and 1930s. The Ocean View Hotel frequently hosted dances for locals.

EARLY PLAYS BY LOCAL RESIDENTS. Plays put on by community members were an important part of life in Davenport in the 1920s and 1930s. After a long day's work in the cement plant and quarry, small crowds would meet at the school auditorium for some light-hearted entertainment.

NORTH COAST RUM RUNNERS. With Prohibition in full swing, illicit alcohol transport was a common occurrence along the coast around Davenport. The wild North Coast, with its hidden coves, secret caves, and beaches, provided needed cover for the so-called "rum runners." Many a bottle made its way through the San Vicente Creek tunnel and into town. The Yellowbank beaches, separated by a tunnel (pictured), have also been mentioned in Prohibition lore.

MISS CALIFORNIA AND A.E. MORELLI, 1924. According to *Notes from Santa Cruz* by Frank Perry, "Mr. Morelli pioneered the local artichoke industry, and as a member of the Santa Cruz Chamber of Commerce, helped bring the first Miss California contest to Santa Cruz." Here, Miss California 1924, Faye Lanphier, pays a visit to the dairymen of the area.

"SONG OF THE ALPS," 1930. Aquilino Ettore Morelli, a busy dairyman by day, also found time to compose many musical scores, reminiscent of his early life in Switzerland. "Song of the Alps," "For You've Lived and Fought," and "Love, Wedding and Lullabies" are a few of the songs that the Morelli family would have enjoyed listening to in the evenings at their home.

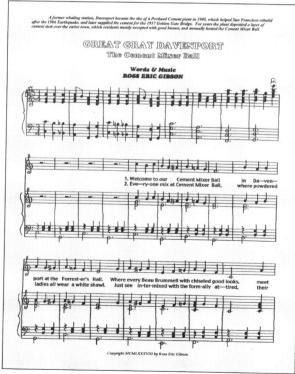

"GREAT GRAY DAVENPORT." Davenport's cement plant inspired Santa Cruz musician and composer Ross Eric Gibson to write a song called "Great Gray Davenport: The Cement Mixer Ball." Gibson wrote another song titled "On The Ghost Coast," where "You'll always raise your spirits the most on the haunting and romantic Ghost Coast!" (Courtesy of Ross Eric Gibson.)

60

Sudden Jim Silent Film, **1917.** Several films have been shot in the Davenport area. *Sudden Jim*, believed to be shot in the San Vicente canyon, centered around love and a logging mill. This scene shows the bridge collapsing behind the train.

The Girl of the Timber Claims, **1917.** Constance Talmadge starred as a young woman protecting her family's timber claim against claim jumpers trying to steal their property. Many key scenes were filmed at the San Vicente logging camp and Gregory Ranch. (Courtesy of Jerry Murbach.)

THE ROMANCE OF ROSY RIDGE,
1947. Lights, camera, poison oak!
The hero, Van Johnson, engages
in a fight with costar Jim Davis.
Johnson would soon be rolling down
a hill covered in poison oak. He
spent three days recovering in the
hospital. Johnson was later quoted
saying, "How could one help but enjoy
working in this wonderful country?
It has been a distinct pleasure from
first to last. The people have been
fine—so have the young folks—their
interest has been an inspiration."
(Courtesy of Alamy Stock Photos.)

JANET LEIGH, 1947. *The Romance
of Rosy Ridge* was Janet Leigh's first
film, at age 19. Lorraine LoBianco of
Turner Classic Movies writes that in
one scene, she was to milk Bessie the
cow: "Bessie wasn't pleased with me at
all and proceeded to step on my foot—
all fifteen hundred pounds of her. It
seemed not to be my day. But it was!
It was a glorious day! It was a perfect
day!" (Courtesy of Jerry Murbach.)

MISS ARTICHOKE, 1924. While Marilyn Monroe was the first "official" California Artichoke Queen in Castroville in 1949, local resident Leonora Garaventa was given the honor of Miss Artichoke 25 years earlier, in Davenport. In the early 1920s, artichokes were one of the region's newest and most lucrative crops, and locals thoroughly enjoyed participating in these lighthearted celebrations. (Courtesy of Josephine Merlotti DiTano.)

MISS ARTICHOKE PARADE FLOAT, 1924. Residents often entered floats in Santa Cruz parades. However, from time to time, they closed the main road in Davenport and held their own local parades. Before World War II, automobile traffic was sparse and hardly a concern on the old Coast Road. Here, Miss Artichoke graces a parade float, surrounded by her royal entourage and a few freshly picked artichokes. (Courtesy of Josephine Merlotti DiTano.)

ALLAN MCLEAN PRINTING SEASIDE REPORTER, 1947. Allan McLean writes, "The *Seaside Reporter* began as a money making scheme. I was desirous of having a twenty-two rifle like the one my older brother had, but was informed that I would have to earn the money for it myself. I was eleven years old. My mother [Hulda McLean] and I came up with the idea of a local news sheet." She would help gather local news and gossip from neighbors and her sewing circle, while Allan wrote about nature and collected stories from the younger residents. He was also responsible for soliciting advertisements from local businesses for the publication. This photograph shows Allan printing the paper on a mimeograph machine. After just two editions, the *Seaside Reporter* had become so successful that residents were submitting material for the paper from as far south as Watsonville and north to Pescadero. (Courtesy of Allan McLean.)

SEASIDE REPORTER

A NEWSPAPER FOR THE FAMILY
October 14, 1947

Vol. 1

No. 18

AIRPLANE CRASHES ON MIRAMAR RANCH

Friday Oct 3 a navy training plane crashed on Joe Scaroni's field between the highway and the beach. Both airmen, Ensign R. W. Koller of Alameda, and Army Leit W. J. Cunningham of Oakland, were killed.

Men working in adjoining fields had heard the motor splutter and go out and then saw the plane spiral to earth where it hit with a crash, dug a hole in the field and exploded into small pieces all over the place.

MINOR COLLISION ON LAST CHANCE ROAD

Mrs. Doll Jackson in her car, collided with Mr. Jackson in the truck on the narrow Last Chance road last week. Mrs. Jackson Sr hit her head against the windshield and broke the windshield of the car.

DAVENPORT CENTER HOLDS ELECTIONS FRIDAY

Davenport Center of Santa Cruz County Farm Bureau will meet Friday Oct. 17 at the Pacific School at 8 p.m. to elect officers and make plans for the coming year.

All members, and farmers interested in farm bureau program are invited to attend. A Center in this area with an interested membership could accomplish a lot for the community and themselves. Among problems that need working out here are: better roads, extension of power service, more adequate telephone service, better rural health facilities, better public and school bus service, neater city garbage disposal, safe and entertaining recreation for young people, better participation in community affairs, lower cost of supplies to farmers, better marketing conditions for farm products, etc.

WADDELL CLIFFS ROAD STILL PASSABLE AFTER RAINS

Eaton and Smith will keep a guide car and adequate equipment on the Waddell Cliffs road all winter, the report, to see that cars can get through. The road was a bit muddy and slippery after the last rain, but not bad. In fact, while waiting for the hourly traffic break, mud is much preferable to the dust we had all summer.

Main hazard to drivers on the Coast Highway is now longer the topheavy cement trucks from Davenport, but the huge truckloads of rip rap rocks on their way to the Waddell road. It is not fun to be stuck behind a truckload stalled on the Scott's Creek Hill, or to pass a load and see ton boulders teetering above one.

SEASIDE SCHOOL RENOVATED

Saturdays Sept 27 and October 11 were work days at Seaside School. The school buzzed with activity as people painted, carpented and plumbered and had a picnic lunch.

The trustees thank Mr. and Mrs. Doll Jackson, Miss Anne Atkins, Miss Fay Bernard, Mrs. Henry Bradley, Mrs. Miriam Cushing, Mr. Joe Gianone, Mr. Charles McLean, Henry, Betsy, and David Bradley, Charles, Allan, and Robbie MacLean, for working so hard.

The school looks lovely painted blue inside with red and white checked curtains and faucets that work.

PROBABILITY OF INCREASE IN DAVENPORT BUS FARE

Southern Pacific Railroad has petitioned the State Public Utilities commision to increase fares (cont. p. 2)

THE SEASIDE REPORTER, 1947. Allan McLean wrote a column about nature and the news from his "younger set," while his mother helped gather items of interest from the Swanton Sewing Circle and neighbors: "Myrtle, the Davenport Postmistress, gave us all the local printable scuttlebutt." At its peak, McLean was distributing around 500 issues twice a month. The young boy was interviewed by larger newspapers in Santa Cruz, San Mateo, and San Francisco. He wrote, "I was invited to, and gave, the pre-keynote speech at the National Amateur Press biennial convention in L.A. in 1948. It was heady stuff for a twelve year-old. And, I got my rifle." As Allan entered high school, his interests shifted away from the little newspaper. He recalls that sports, cars, and girls began to consume most of his spare time, and the *Seaside Reporter* was no more. (Courtesy of Allan McLean.)

RELIGIOUS INSTRUCTION, 1962.
According to a March 12, 1962,
Santa Cruz Sentinel article by Wallace
Trabing, "Davenport school youngsters
set off from the Pacific School
to the Catholic church for their
weekly hour of religious instruction."
Protestant students met in a building
behind the Mira Mar bar, where
today's Whale City cafe is located.
(Photograph by Wallace Trabing.)

FULL GOSPEL CHURCH, 1962. Located next to Lundberg Studios on the Old Coast Road, this home-based church was known for its outside speakers and a 600-pound pig named Ellis. Rev. Albert J. Poole led English and Spanish services from 1956 into the 1960s. Reverend Poole was known for his outgoing, neighborly personality, and so was the pig. The building survives and is now a private residence. (Photograph by Ruth-Marion Baruch, courtesy of UCSC Special Collections and Archives.)

JOE BROVIA, 1955. Born in Davenport in 1922, Joe Brovia had a baseball contract in hand before he finished high school. Between 1941 and 1955, he was a star outfielder for the Pacific Coast League's San Francisco Seals, Portland Beavers, Sacramento Solons, and the Oakland Oaks. In 1955, he played in the majors with the Cincinnati Redlegs. Brovia dazzled crowds with his left-handed power hits, which launched baseballs well out of ballparks.

JOE BROVIA FAN CLUB, 1950s. In 1947, Brovia hit a 560-foot home run over a 40-foot-high fence in Seals Stadium. His remarkable batting and six-foot, three-inch frame earned him the nicknames "Big Slugger," "Joltin-Joe," and "the Davenport Destroyer." The local Joe Brovia fan club organized bus trips to area games to support their hometown hero. Brovia was inducted into both the Italian Hall of Fame and the Pacific Coast League Hall of Fame.

JUBILEE SQUARE DANCERS BANNER, 1950s. Square dancing was a popular pastime in Davenport. The Jubilee Squares held dances at the school and competed with other square dancing groups in the area. Children came along as well and were looked after in one of the unoccupied classrooms nearby. (Courtesy of Leon Gregory.)

PICNICS AT LAGUNA GROVE, 1950s. Swiss Italian gatherings drew visitors to the Davenport area from as far as San Francisco for a day of celebration. Author Alverda Orlando remembers one such picnic with close to 1,000 people in attendance. The Get Together Orchestra frequently entertained crowds at these gatherings. It was not a party unless there was dancing involved. (Photograph by Kramer.)

LOCAL DANCES, 1960s. Community dances were held in local hotels, Forester's Hall, and the school auditorium. Refreshments were served at 11:00 p.m. during the orchestra's break. Children often fell asleep on chairs pushed together, snugly wrapped in their parent's discarded coats and jackets. On one occasion, a child dropped coins down into an electrical outlet and shorted out the entire venue—lights out!

DAVENPORT NIGHT, 1961. To raise money for the volunteer fire department, the community held a firemen's ball at Pacific School. According to the *Santa Cruz Sentinel*, "Behind the wheel is the general chairman, Davenport's unofficial mayor, Elio Orlando, with [author] Mrs. Alverda Orlando, Mrs. Larry DiTano, Mrs. Albert Novelli, DiTano and Novelli." (Courtesy of *Santa Cruz Sentinel*.)

ELIO ORLANDO, PAGEANT OF PIONEERS, 1967. On the grassy knoll overlooking the coast, Elio Orlando', author Alverda Orlando's husband, participated in the Pageant of Pioneers. He had never ridden a horse before this day. Reenacting the history of the area, he posed as John Davenport spotting whales in the distance. It is unknown whether Captain Davenport owned a horse, but it was a nice shot for the local papers.

THE WHALE SIGN, 1983. Davenport hosted gray whale celebrations from the 1960s into the 1980s. Many versions of large whale signs appeared over the years. Most ended up being burned in beach bonfires. To drum up excitement, contests were held for the best photograph of the sign. Here, Alvin Gregory and Dave Maars, the Lonestar cement plant manager, are most likely pretending to see a whale. (Courtesy of *Santa Cruz Sentinel*.)

Six

THE 1920s AND 1930s

MOCETTINI DAIRY, 2011. The North Coast dairies continued to prosper during the 1920s, but the coming of the Depression and new sanitary regulations made it increasingly difficult to operate dairies on the coast. Many of the early dairies were unable to afford the costs associated with the new requirements and slowly faded away. Situated adjacent to Agua Puerca Creek, this dairy structure survives on Cement Plant Road, previously Old Coast Highway. This property is now managed by the Bureau of Land Management.

VENEZIA HOTEL, DAVENPORT LANDING. The 1913 fire destroyed all businesses on the ocean side of Davenport Landing, including the Venezia hotel. This photograph shows the rebuilt hotel in the early 1920s. The Venezia suffered a final blow in 1924 when yet another fire claimed the building.

BEACH COTTAGES, DAVENPORT LANDING. The boom at Davenport Landing continued into the early 1880s, but due to the lack of reliable shipping facilities, the village's population began to decline. In time, after the wharves were gone and the fires had destroyed most of the town's buildings, Davenport Landing became a small community of homes with a county-managed beach park.

NARROW GAUGE ELECTRIC LOCOMOTIVE, 1924. In 1923, the Standard Portland Cement Company purchased an entire narrow gauge railroad from the Alaska Gastineau Mining Company to replace the standard gauge equipment used for haulage between the quarry and the main plant. The new equipment consisted of two 18-ton overhead-wire electric locomotives, 60 rock cars, and 3 or 4 battery locomotives. At the quarry, the four battery locomotives shuttled mine cars around the area. This equipment was lighter, cleaner, and a lot quieter.

QUARRY "GLORY HOLE," 1920s. The quarry employed a unique underground transport system where limestone was blasted away from the cliffs into a steep funnel-shaped pit, which fed rock into rail cars in the tunnel below. Sixteen holes like this one were created during the life of the quarry. This method of mining originated in the gold mines and was unique in the cement industry at this time. The quarrymen pictured are using pneumatic drills. (Courtesy of Robert W. Piwarzyk.)

CEMENT BAG STACKER, 1930S. Most cement was transported in bags and barrels before the 1930s, when bulk methods first began to be utilized. Santa Cruz Portland cement was marketed as the Blue Cross brand, with bags weighing 94 pounds, the same weight Portland cement is sold today.

PIER BEING BUILT, 1934. With cement demand strong, construction began on a pier to ship bulk finished product to storage facilities up and down the coast. The welded steel pier was a bold move considering previous wharf failures and notorious winter waves. A pile driver drove the metal pilings deep into the bedrock. Building a wharf in the middle of the winter proved challenging when large waves damaged the pier and sent the pile driver overboard. (Courtesy of Ross Eric Gibson.)

SS SANTACRUZCEMENT AND FINISHED WHARF, 1930s. The world's first cement tanker, this ship was outfitted specifically to carry cement. The ship was loaded by a massive compressor, forcing cement from the storage silos through two 12-inch pipes. The ship was moored carefully and connected to the pipes at the end of the wharf with a flexible hose. Capacity was around 45,000 barrels of bulk, plus sack cement. For over 15 years, product was efficiently transported using this method. During World War II, the SS *SantaCruzCement* delivered countless tons of cement to Hawaii for military infrastructure. In 1954, after storms had severely damaged the pier, the ship was sold, and product was then moved by truck and railroad.

DAVENPORT SERVICE STATION, 1925. Albert Gregory's service station plans were drawn up by the same architect who designed Davenport's new school. Albert's son Alvin recalled, "Gregory's Service Station opened in 1925, just before the school did. There were few cars then, mostly horse and wagons. Some days he didn't service a single car. In 1930, we changed over to Gilmore Gasoline."

GREGORY GAS STATION AND THE DAY THE LION CAME, 1930. A lion, pictured in a cage behind the car, was part of an advertising campaign for Gilmore Gasoline. The gas station housed a small cafe that catered mostly to cement plant workers, and a convenience store section toward the back of the restaurant. Sons Alvin and Francis eventually took over the family business.

PIERCE ARROW, 1933. Fire was always on the minds of Davenport residents. In August 1933, a second-hand Pierce Arrow was purchased and renovated into the town's first fire truck. Its 100-gallon tank had a hose suitable for extinguishing small fires. The purchase of this truck was made possible by the artichoke ranchers near Davenport.

OVERLAND FIRE ENGINE, 1934. In 1934, a somewhat larger Overland passenger car was purchased and renovated into Davenport's second fire truck. Fire Chief Frank Meyer, standing at left, organized fire drills and demonstrations and offered first-aid training for the town's volunteer force. During World War II, when many of the men were away, firefighting duties fell to the old-timers.

VINTAGE CRATE LABELS. The cool, moist coastal climate proved a perfect environment for growing Brussels sprouts and artichokes. Sprouts were first cultivated in Davenport in 1915 by A. Puccinelli. In 1916, Aquilino Ettore Morelli planted 52 artichoke plants as an experimental crop in the Davenport area. The artichokes thrived, and local farmers quickly realized the crop's financial potential. Sprouts and artichokes are still dominant crops today.

ARTICHOKE FIELDS, 1930s. The globe artichoke, originally introduced to California by Spanish immigrants in the 1880s, was especially treasured by the local Italian immigrant population who were both landowners and field workers. The first fieldworkers in the area were Italians. Filipino and Mexican immigrants joined them in the 1920s. Old labor camp buildings can still be seen along the coast.

A.E. Morelli Packing Shed. Davenport became one of the largest producers of artichokes in California. Upscale restaurants across the country began adding the exotic and expensive California artichoke to their menus. Other locally grown produce included lima beans, broccoli, cauliflower, peas, and rhubarb. The packing plants offered residents seasonal employment as well as an opportunity to reconnect with friends and catch up on local gossip.

Packing Plant Employees, 1940s. Bags of slightly bruised or imperfect produce were one of the perks of working at the packing shed. At the end of the day, the produce was packed in ice and shipped off on a waiting train. Author Alverda Orlando remembers her mother taking a leave of absence from her day job at Gregory's station to work at the packing plant. Like many workers, she would simply resume her job after the harvest season was over.

AERIAL VIEW OF DAVENPORT, 1930s. The Standard Portland Cement Company can be seen below the smoke at center. Old Town, along with the main San Vicente Creek watershed, sits off to the right. On the left bordering the ocean are agricultural fields that sit across the road from New Town. The top and center of the photograph show the ruggedness of the land and most of the original quarries.

CROCKER HOSPITAL AND CLINIC, 1939. Due to frequent accidents, the cement plant built a hospital in 1910. The Crocker Hospital was financed by William Crocker, founder of Crocker Banks and one of the principal financiers of the cement plant. The hospital offered a six-bed ward complete with surgical facilities. Dr. Gainor stands in front of the hospital in this 1939 photograph. It was closed in the 1940s and was used by Cal Fire in the 1960s and 1970s.

HOTEL D'ITALIA, 1940s. By the 1940s, the large, rambling Hotel D'Italia was no longer on the main road running through town. In 1939, the Ocean Shore Highway (Highway 1) was completed and bypassed this section of town. Although the hotel was open to all visitors, the Hotel D'Italia originally housed a large number of quarry workers and was later home to Mexican and Filipino farm laborers. A fire tore through the hotel on December 17, 1945, and reduced it to ashes.

CAIOCCA AND SONS DAVENPORT BAKERY, 1930s. After working at the cement plant for 15 years, Gilbert Caiocca became part owner of the D'Italia hotel and, in 1922, founded the Davenport Bakery, baking breads in the building now used by Lundberg Studios for blowing glass. Working with his sons Bill and Leo, the business expanded to the new building seen here in 1937, where they also ran a grocery, deli, and a gas station. When his sons Bill and Leo entered the war, the bakery closed for the duration. Henry Molfino purchased the business in 1946.

Seven

THE WAR AND AFTER

WORLD WAR II TROOPS, 1942. During World War II, soldiers were stationed all along the California coast. A contingent from the all-black 54th Coast Artillery was dispatched to the Santa Cruz area, and the troops seen here were stationed at the Davenport hospital. In an effort to keep troop movements secret, residents were occasionally evacuated from their homes for the duration of military exercises. Sometimes, residents would climb the hillside under the gun emplacements, where they had excellent views of the troop movements below.

GIANONE HILL LOOKOUT, EARLY 1940S. California coastal residents were put on high alert following the December 1941 attack on Pearl Harbor. Believing that the Japanese might attack the mainland at any time, lookouts were constructed. Frank McCrary Sr. built the spotter's cabin at left. Helen Gianone is holding a telescope provided by Theodore Hoover, area resident and brother of former president Herbert Hoover. (Courtesy of the McCrary family.)

FRANK "LUD" MCCRARY JR., C. 1941. One evening in February 1942, two local boys, Lud McCrary and Dick West, were posted at the lookout on Gianone Hill when they spotted something in the waters near Davenport. The boys saw unusual lights flickering offshore and thought it could be a Japanese submarine. They immediately called the Bay Area military authorities and reported the strange sighting. (Courtesy of the McCrary family.)

"I" Series Japanese Submarine, c. 1941. An airplane from the Army Air Corps rushed to the area off Davenport and exchanged fire with the vessel, a Japanese submarine thought to be I-17. Launched before the Pacific war began, nine "I" series Japanese submarines were sent to bomb the United States. Initial plans called for the shelling of San Francisco on Christmas day 1941, but plans changed, and the submarines were called to other positions along the West Coast.

Pilot Mike Demos, 1942. When Davenport resident and Army pilot Mike Demos came home on leave, he would fly very low and greet his hometown by dipping his wings. Area children, who could not contain their excitement, ran from their homes and school to wave at his passing plane. According to nephew Leon Gregory, Demos was a fighter pilot who fought in the battles of Guadalcanal and Midway. (Courtesy of Leon Gregory.)

PACIFIC SCHOOL, 1926. This school was built in 1924 on a parcel of land provided by Coast Dairies and Land Company. The cement used for the project was donated by the local plant. Because the building could not meet earthquake safety requirements, it was bulldozed by the Lone Star Cement Corporation in 1978, and a new school was built. This process took about four years from planning to opening day, during which students were taught in temporary buildings around town.

NEW PACIFIC SCHOOL. Davenport's new school, built in 1978, houses kindergarten through sixth-grade students who enjoy unique programming such as Life Lab and Food Lab. Older students take on greater responsibilities such as composting, planting, harvesting, measuring, recording, and planning experiments. Fifth and sixth graders assist in preparing school lunches, including cooking, menu planning, and nutritional analysis. All students benefit from the Pacific School's commitment to a well-rounded, hands-on, project-based education.

ELECTRIC PASSENGER CAR, 1942. The cement plant bought a scrapped passenger car in 1942 to transport quarry workers. The car was refurbished with wooden benches, which could seat up to 35 men. It was said that for fun, the men would place bets to see how fast the car could go. The operator would open the controller and rush to the back, and the driverless car would hurtle downhill. Finally braking before reaching the bottom, the car then drifted nonchalantly past the plant manager.

SOUTHERN PACIFIC TRAIN AND DAVENPORT STATION. Older students in Davenport had to travel by train to Santa Cruz to attend high school. Sal Celebrado remembers the trips well: "It was a pretty good ride, but it wasn't very fast. I imagine about twenty to twenty-five miles per hour. We got dropped off at Bay and California Street. From there we walked to the high school." Pictured is a tourist train arriving at Davenport in the 1940s or 1950s. (Courtesy of Covello and Covello.)

EVOLUTION OF THE CEMENT PLANT, 1960s. Over the years, the changing owners of the cement plant faced numerous legal actions and complaints related to air and noise pollution from farmers, residents, and businesses. Upgrades were initiated to mitigate the harmful impacts and increase efficiency and quality of product. By the early 1980s, the worst of the dust fallout was over, but the use of coal as an energy source and the very nature of the process meant that many environmental and health issues remained.

BELTLINE CONVEYOR SYSTEM, 1972. With the opening of the new Bonny Doon quarry in 1969, rather than relying on trains or road transport, a new, more efficient conveyor belt system was built to transport raw limestone nearly four miles from the quarry and across Bonny Doon Road to the plant. The old San Vicente quarry with its glory holes, tunnels, and trains was history. The dismantling of the conveyor began in 2016 for use at another facility. (Courtesy of Lonestar Materials.)

DUSTED CAR, C. 1950S. Dust from the cement plant settled over the little town. The tops of automobiles, fences, roofs, roads, and lawns were covered in a layer of dust from the night before. Local children remember making footprints on the sidewalks as they walked to school, and laundry left to dry on the clotheslines would become cement sculpture if left too long under the gray skies of Davenport.

DAVENPORT EGGS. Before easy access to Santa Cruz, all homes had large backyards where vegetables were grown and chickens thrived. The Davenport housewife had to have a strong wrist to crack the eggs, as the shells were nearly as hard as a snail's. For better or worse, local chickens pecked the ground and ingested lime and cement dust, which created extremely hard shells. (Courtesy of Leah Lambert.)

HIGHWAY 1 AND THE BUSINESS DISTRICT, 1950s. The post office was still in the Cash Store when this 1950s photograph was taken. The building third from left housed a bar called the Mira Mar Inn, later the Whaler. Davenport's Highway 1 location provided plenty of customers for the gas stations, bars, accommodations, and stores that lined the highway. The two gas station franchises shown here were Mobil and Shell.

SPORTSMAN'S
RETREAT

DAVENPORT
CALIF.

W-89
© Webber
1950

OCEAN VIEW HOTEL, 1950. Through the years, weary travelers, fishermen, hunters, and locals enjoyed the hospitality and quality food at this iconic hotel. With a well-stocked bar and room to dance, the Bella family provided fun and entertainment for the town. In 1960, the Bellas sold the hotel to the Monti family, who extensively remodeled it in 1961. One year later, a fire completely destroyed the building.

THE GREAT DAVENPORT CASH STORE FIRE, 1953. On the morning of March 22, 1953, the Cash Store, post office, and notary office were engulfed in flames. The tiny Davenport fire department was powerless against the raging fire, and the building was lost. They were able to keep the flames from spreading to adjoining buildings until other fire departments could get to the scene. Ammunition that had been stored in the attic of the Cash Store ignited, and bullets flew. Bystanders reported hearing the rounds exploding and bullets ricocheting through the building and across the street. One resident reported that when she reached home hours later, she noticed a bullet had torn through her scarf. Luckily there were no injuries, as the store was closed at the time of the fire. After this, residents raised money to build a firehouse and petitioned Santa Cruz County to create a fire district in the area.

CASH STORE VAULT, 1953. The Cash Store's cement walls and vault withstood the 1953 fire, and with no immediate plans for rebuilding the store, the concrete ruins remained for many years. When the neighboring Ocean View Hotel burned, also damaging Forester's Hall, this section of town resembled a dusty ghost town.

DAVENPORT AVENUE, 1960s. Davenport Avenue has always been loved for its simple cabin architecture. Most of the early homes had Italian-style nine-foot ceilings. The building on the left is the vacant meat market, and the second house from the right was Dorello Morelli's residence. The St. Vincent de Paul Church sits at the end of the block.

MEAT MARKET, 1969. The photograph below looks out from inside the ruins of the meat market Joe Bourche built in 1907. Subsequent owners included James Cuclis (Kouklakis), Leonidas Marinos, and Hugo Bagnasco. Cuclis, born on Crete, worked for two years in the quarry before becoming a partner in the Coast Dairies and Land Company. Across the street is the abandoned blacksmith shop built by Alex Luittrel that later became Celebrado's Auto Repair. The meat market was severely damaged in a fire in 1936. At right is an ad for the Coast Meat Market under the ownership of Bagnasco and Marinos.

COAST MEAT MARKET
BAGNASCO and MARINOS, Props.
Phone 4-Y-15
DAVENPORT, CALIF.

NEW POST OFFICE, 1953. Myrtle Garaventa was the Davenport postmaster at the time of the great Cash Store fire. Legend has it that she rushed into the burning building to rescue the still-unopened mailbag. A policeman at the scene questioned her authority, as he had never heard of a woman postmaster before. After being detained in his squad car for a short while, Garaventa was deposited along with the mailbag outside of the Ocean View Hotel. Pictured is the opening of the new post office with Davenport entrepreneur Alvin Gregory presenting the flowers.

GREGORY'S DEPARTMENT STORE, LATE 1950s. In 1957, Alvin and Francis Gregory purchased the post office building and opened a men's and boys' clothing and small appliance store, expanding beyond the gas station, general store, and lunch counter business next door. The Gregorys were also very active in the community. Alvin was a county supervisor for eight years, and Francis was a member of the local school board.

MOBILE HOME PARK PROPOSAL, LATE 1950s. The Surf Side Resort was comprised of a string of small cottages along the beach at Davenport Landing. Charles Powell purchased the buildings two days before one cottage burned to the ground, only to be followed by a second fire months later. Powell had plans to rebuild Davenport Landing with a trailer court, motel, and other businesses. He protested the environmental effects of the cement plant by displaying several large signs on his property, pictured here.

HAIR-CUTTING DAY, EARLY 1960s. Reynaldo "Pancho" Perez is seen giving his sons haircuts. Joe Perez is in the chair, with Filo and Rey Perez Jr. looking on. Perez, a native of northeast Mexico, worked as a mason at the cement plant for 32 years. He is well known for having purchased all his children houses on the same road near San Vicente Creek. It is said he negotiated good prices by letting the Italian sellers live out their lives in the homes.

DAVENPORT JAIL, LATE 1950s. As early as 1958, the county decided to sell the jail. In 1961, Santa Cruz County advertised Davenport's jailhouse in the local paper. It was sold to Jess Carothers for $110, who used it as a storage shed. The jail was later sold to Susanne Poett who, it was rumored, had considered making the jail into a seaside retreat. Instead, the little jail sat vacant for years.

BELLA VISTA LANDSLIDE, 1962. On March 7, 1962, most of the village of Bella Vista was lost in a massive landslide. Quarry workers heard the rumbling from the mine and rushed toward their homes. Fortunately, during the time of the landslide, the children were on their way home from school and their parents were at work. Amazingly, no deaths occurred from this disaster.

FORESTER'S HALL, 1970s. Built in 1915, Forester's Hall was a popular spot for dances, plays, card parties, graduations, and other programs. Movies were also shown here on Friday or Saturday nights. The building had not been used since the 1950s. In 1997, after much debate, the county reluctantly approved demolition with the owner's commitment to recreate the facade when rebuilt. The newly restored jail can be seen behind the hall.

OCEAN VIEW STEAKHOUSE, EARLY 1970s. This restaurant was next to the post office in a building owned by the Gregorys that has seen quite a few businesses come and go. Bill Williamson owned and ran this restaurant until 1975. He sold it to Clyde and Jacqueline McGuire, who turned it into Jackie's Coffee Shop from 1975 through 1977. (Courtesy of Frank Perry.)

DAVENPORT FIRE DEPARTMENT, 1970. The Santa Cruz Chamber of Commerce presented the Davenport Fire Department with the Men of the Year award for their ocean and cliff rescue work. From humble beginnings, the all-volunteer force has grown from a small group of hardworking, concerned citizens into a full-fledged, professional fire department.

ANIMAL RESCUE VEST, 1972. Davenport's crumbling cliffs would often take an unsuspecting tourist and sometimes their four-legged companion over a precipice. Canine cliff rescues were also part of the Davenport Fire Department's duties. In this photograph, a local firefighter's patient pooch models a harness used in such recoveries.

REFILLING TANK FROM SAN VICENTE CREEK, 1974. This fire engine was a gift from the City of Santa Cruz and was sold to the Davenport Fire Department for one dollar in April 1974. Manufactured by Van Pelt of Oakdale, California, it had a 500-gallon tank, which could be refilled at the local creek. With a tank capacity five times larger than the force's older model, the truck was a serious upgrade for the department.

EVOLUTION OF THE PACKING SHED. Louis Poletti's 13,000-square-foot Davenport Producers shed was purchased and saved from ruin by Fred and Bren Bailey in 1960. In 1986, fresh juice entrepreneurs Greg Steltenpohl and Steve Williamson moved their Odwalla juice operation into the shed. Juice production moved to the Central Valley in 1994, but research at the "drink tank" continued at Davenport until 1998. Odwalla was purchased by Coca-Cola in 2001. Other tenants have included Interplanetary Soles and Save the Waves.

EL JARRO POINT, 1979. With Davenport Landing on the right, this aerial photograph shows a portion of the Coast Dairies land that was lease-optioned by Pacific Gas and Electric to build the largest nuclear plant complex in the world. With pressure mounting from diverse groups and a newly discovered active fault, the plans were withdrawn in 1977. (Courtesy of Kenneth and Gabrielle Adelman, California Coastal Records Project.)

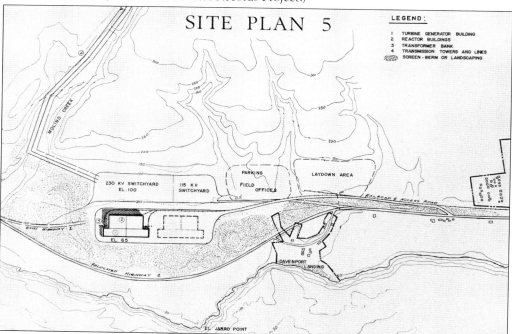

PROPOSED SITE PLAN FOR NUCLEAR PLANT, EARLY 1970s. This plan depicts a phase-one option that would have placed two reactors on Highway 1, rerouting the highway closer to the ocean. Mitigating visibility concerns was considered key to gaining support. Four more reactors were to be constructed, bringing the output to over six million kilowatts. A harbor and jetty were also planned to support material and machinery transport and recreation. (Courtesy of Santa Cruz City Library.)

Eight

ARTS AND CRAFTY

DAVENPORT TRAIN DEPOT BY DOLLY GREGORY, 1975. Dolly Gregory, a Santa Cruz native and wife of Alvin Gregory, worked at the couple's store in Davenport. They met at the 4-H Club at Pacific School. Her paintings were often seen around town. This one depicts the Southern Pacific Railroad train station that used to sit just north of town.

RANCHO DEL OSO BY HULDA HOOVER MCLEAN. McLean's uncle was former president Herbert Hoover, and her father was a Stanford University dean. "She was an enormously talented person. She painted, she wrote, and she was involved in politics," said Barbara McCrary, who had known McLean for 55 years. McLean was one of Santa Cruz County's first female supervisors and spent many years at her family's Waddell Creek ranch, 11 miles north of Davenport. (Courtesy of George Fox University.)

AEOLUS BOAT SHOP. For over 40 years, Bill Grunwald built boats in the old Hotel D'Italia livery barn by San Vicente Creek. The main hotel burned in 1945, but the barn survived and has been in continuous use for over a century. Grunwald was one of the most established small boat builders in Northern California and specialized in designs dating to the early 1800s. (Courtesy of Joe Ray.)

LUNDBERG STUDIOS, 1970. The late James Lundberg (right) became the first California glass artist to reproduce the colors and patterns of the highly acclaimed Tiffany studios. Founded in a backyard shop, Lundberg Studios today continues to produce collectible art glass with a range of products including vases, scent bottles, paper weights, lighting, and custom commissions. Longtime glassblower Daniel Salazar is seen below working in the factory. To quote Lundberg, "My work and that of my studio is an outgrowth of my love and fascination with glass. The formulations, special tools, and equipment have all been labors of love. I always look into the material for my inspiration. I am a glass man." (Both, courtesy of Rebecca Lundberg.)

BOYE KNIVES. While living in Davenport, David Boye taught himself the craft of knife making, wrote a best-selling book, and discovered the innovative dendritic blade metallurgy. In the early 1970s, Boye made thousands of knives from recycled sawmill blades. He also set a world record by making 3,000 cuts of one-inch hemp rope without any resharpening. Boye is considered one of the fathers of modern knife making. (Courtesy of David Boye.)

REDWOOD SLABS AND THE DAVENPORT MILL, 1970S. In 1974, David Lundberg (kneeling with dog) set up a woodshop and mill next to his brother's glass factory and San Vicente Creek. With more enthusiasm than money, old cast-iron machines—many of them abandoned and rusting—were put to work creating fine custom wood products. Lundberg and crew shared a love for woodcraft and resurrected almost forgotten traditional wood joinery and techniques. (Courtesy of David Lundberg.)

"BONNY DOON BEACH" BY TOM KILLION. This woodcut depicts Bonny Doon Beach, or what was originally Williams Landing, the first landing in the area, about one mile south of Davenport. In the 1970s, Tom Killion lived down by San Vicente Creek, or as he calls it, "the swamp." A master printer who specializes in Japanese woodcuts, Killion worked extensively in the Davenport area. This is a multi-block reduction cut measuring 13 by 19.5 inches. (Courtesy of Tom Killion.)

DARK HORSE POTTERY, 2009. Joel Magen's pottery studio with his backyard kiln was located in New Town on the north edge of town. As one of the few potters in the area to offer an apprenticeship, Magen helped educate many local potters. He was concerned with both the beauty and the functionality of pottery and always kept an eye to both in his vases, lamps, funerary jars, cups, and bowls. (Photograph by Ward Coffey.)

BILL FRAVEL WATERCOLORS. A Santa Cruz native, Bill Fravel relocated to Davenport in 1994 and set up an ocean-view art studio, the WhaleHedge, named after the large shrub topiary he shaped bordering the studio. For the next 12 years, he offered workshops and produced award-winning watercolors inspired by the places and people of this wild coast. The fine art and ambiance of the WhaleHedge studio were featured in print media across the country. (Courtesy of Susan Hancy.)

BUD BOGLE FURNITURE SHOP. Since 1987, Bud Bogle has been building functional, one-of-a-kind furniture out of his backyard shop in New Town. Known for his high level of craftsmanship, Bogle employs exotic and local woods and does his own upholstery using European and domestic fine leathers. His output includes rockers, loveseats, sofas, tables, dining chairs, and stools. He opens the doors to visitors during select events throughout the year. (Photograph by Ed Dickie.)

DAVENPORT GALLERY, 2011. Founded by Roger Knapp in 2010, the Davenport Gallery was a popular stop for highway travelers and locals alike. The gallery supported local talent with private gallery space and themed monthly shows that allowed nonmembers to exhibit. Talented artists and musicians, far too many to name, live along the coast and in the hills. The gallery closed in 2012, with the space now a tasting room for Bonny Doon Vineyard. (Photograph by Roy Moore.)

HOMEGROWN SURFBOARDS, 2010. Around 2009, Local artist and surfer Nef (Neftali Espino) opened a surf shop in the Whale City historic auxiliary building where he sold custom surfboards, art, and surf paraphernalia. He was a renowned board shaper. The vibe was typical of the rootsy surf culture found along this coast. (Photograph by Ed Dickie.)

DAVENPORT SURF AND SAIL, 2019. Joe Ray took over the Hotel D'Italia livery stable soon after Bill Grunwald passed away in 1998. Local winds fuel some of the best sailboarding on the coast, and Joe Ray has mended sails and provided gear for over three decades. He lays the sails out on huge tables in a building that has been a home for blacksmiths, mechanics, boat makers, horses, and more. (Photograph by Ed Dickie.)

Nine

THE DUST CLEARS

NEW CASH STORE, 1977. After the Cash Store burned down, the land sat empty for years. Pictured here is the New Davenport Cash Store just after completion in 1977. Bruce and Marcia McDougal initially just wanted a place for their pottery students to live and sell what they produced, but it became an eclectic gift shop paired with a restaurant and bed-and-breakfast. In 2007, a collective of locals extensively remodeled and upgraded the premises and renamed it the Davenport Roadhouse at the Cash Store. In 2013, Helmut John Fritz and Queenie purchased the business and renamed it the Davenport Roadhouse Restaurant and Inn. (Courtesy of Marcia McDougal.)

DAVENPORT POSTMASTERS. Formerly Myrtle Steele of the pioneer family of San Mateo County, Myrtle Garaventa (right) was Davenport postmaster from 1937 to 1979. After a brief period with Jean Peterson and George Sather at the helm, Maria (Perez) Olivas (left) took over the job. She is a life-long resident and active member in the community. Previous postmasters include Louis Poletti, Dorello Morelli, and Mary V. Pooley. The post office has always been the social center of town.

JIM FRANKS JR. AND SUE WILSON, 1980. According to a *Santa Cruz Sentinel* article from September 24, 1980, fourteen-year-old Jim Franks Jr. planned and supervised the renovation of the Davenport jail for his Eagle Scout project. The proposed budget was $700, but due to years of neglect, the cost to repair the jail grew to double that amount. In true Davenport fashion, residents pitched in and donated many hours to the cause. (Courtesy of the *Santa Cruz Sentinel*.)

DAVENPORT RESOURCE SERVICE CENTER OPENING, 1985. As part of the Community Action Board of Santa Cruz County, the Davenport Resource Service Center (DRSC) partners with the community to eliminate poverty and create social change through advocacy, essential services, and celebration. With roots going back to the national War On Poverty in 1964, the DRSC was founded in 1977, working out of trailers until a permanent home was built in 1985. (Courtesy of the DRSC.)

NEW DAVENPORT FIRE STATION, 1991. With funds and donated land from Lone Star Cement, a new fire station was built in 1991 without any taxpayer money. Local residents and businesses also contributed money, labor, and materials. Moving from the cramped 700-square-foot space at Pacific School, the new home was a major upgrade. Davenport volunteer firefighters are part of the Santa Cruz County Fire Department. The building is also used for community meetings and elections.

THE MAYOR, 2011. The little two-cell jail was just 15 feet square, with 8-inch thick walls of solid concrete. Like the church and hospital, the original roof was concrete. There was a small lobby where the sheriff could fill out paperwork. Unofficial town mayors for Davenport have included Louis Moretti, Charles Bella, Elio Orlando, and Noel Bock (pictured), who worked for 25 years as the office manager of the Pacific School. (Photograph by Ed Dickie.)

CLAMPERS REHABILITATING DAVENPORT JAIL, 1980. A group known as the Clampers (the Order of E Clampus Vitus) volunteered their labor and knowledge of building restoration and repaired the deteriorating concrete walls of the Davenport jail. They also installed a French drain to divert water runoff from the roof and nearby hillside. (Courtesy of Jim Cirner.)

DAVENPORT JAIL RESTORED. The jail has been difficult to maintain because of constant corrosion from salt air and moisture. The residents of Davenport loved their little jail and have rallied several times to save it. The building was damaged in the 1989 earthquake to the tune of about $8,000. It was reopened in 1992, but by the end of the 1990s, the Davenport Resource Service Center offered to take it over because it was not being properly cared for. The population held a raucous meeting to "save our jail" from outside influences. After a local resident went to the county board of supervisors to file a complaint, it was discovered that the jail actually belonged to the Museum of Art and History in Santa Cruz, not the town of Davenport. According to the local newspaper, Davenport residents came together once again and began repair work on their historic jail. Thirty-six people, including the director of the Museum of Art and History, gathered at the end of September 20, 2005, to install a new roof on the jail.

A MODERN WHALE TOWN, 2010. With a post office, corner store, restaurants, and hotel, tiny Davenport makes up for its size with bustling activity. The confluence of human activity and stunning natural beauty has revitalized the town and attracts whale watchers, nature lovers, art enthusiasts, and restaurant patrons to the area. Now surrounded by publicly owned and managed lands, the last remaining population growth will come when the cement plant is sold.

CEMEX USA CEMENT PLANT, 2007. The discovery of chromium-6 in the schoolyard initiated a temporary plant closure in 2009. The ongoing recession, environmental issues, increased operational costs, and regulatory pressure all contributed to the final shuttering of the plant in 2010. The facility had been in continuous operation for over a century and defined much of Davenport's identity. With the cement plant no longer contributing to costs and maintenance, water and sewer rates became some of the highest in the country. (Photograph by Pete Johnson.)

THE WHALER, 1990. Following in the tradition of the Mira Mar, the Whaler was a popular bar and burger joint for travelers and locals alike. Reacting to an out of town investor threatening to buy up the town, the McDougals purchased the building from Alvin Gregory in 1982. After the purchase, the Whaler, with peanut-shell floor and Confederate flag, remained the same throughout much of the 1980s. (Courtesy of Carlo Savigni.)

WHALE CITY, 2011. Originally, Whale City served as a gas station and commercial bakery supplying the Cash Store restaurant, but in the early 1990s, with the McDougals' son Kristen Raugust now at the helm, Whale City Bakery Bar and Grill was opened. For almost three decades, Whale City, with its ocean view and international vibe, has been providing a friendly space to slow down and maybe even catch a whale breaching. The nearest gas station is now 10 miles to the south or 15 to the north. (Photograph by Ed Dickie.)

BOAT TIE-DOWN, 2010. The wharves, hotels, saloons, and shops of Davenport Landing are now history. This heavy iron tie-down, or eye bolt, is the last visible remnant of the whaling era. Tie-downs were used to help keep early ships stationary during the loading and unloading process in the rough seas. A similar tie-down can be found near Davenport. (Photograph by Ed Dickie.)

FISH LADDER, DAVENPORT LANDING, 2013. The only ocean ranching operation permitted in California, Silverking Oceanic Farms opened in 1969. Salmon and steelhead were hatched elsewhere and brought to the Davenport Landing facility, acclimated, and sent down the fish ladder to the ocean. The plan was foiled by inadequate numbers of returning fish, so Silverking stopped the operation and explored tank farming. When this option was not viable, the business was sold to US Abalone in the early 1990s. (Photograph by Ed Dickie.)

DAVENPORT LANDING, 2019. Large springtime waves sweep around El Jarro point at "the Landing." The two early wharves were no match for the large waves common to this coast. In the foreground is American Abalone Farms, an aquaculture facility that grows California red abalone with fresh seawater and locally sourced kelp. Due to overfishing, the California abalone industry collapsed in the 1990s. A handful of private residences and a small county park make up the remainder of this historic beach cove. (Photograph by Ed Dickie.)

MOLINO CREEK FARM COLLECTIVE, 2019. This farm community is the central coast's oldest dry-farmed organic tomato grower. It was founded in 1983 by several families to preserve family farming and the beauty of the land. Lewis Chandler had a ranch on this land in the late 1800s, and later, it was called the Greek Ranch. With an elevation of around 1,000 feet, summers have warm days and cool nights for sweeter tomatoes and thriving olive and apple orchards. This plentiful land with ocean views sits adjacent to Molino Creek in the hills just north of Davenport.

DAVENPORT BLUFFS, 2010. The bluffs in front of Davenport have always been a popular place to take in the ocean and maybe spot some whales. In 2001, the Santa Cruz Land Trust acquired a conservation easement from the Cemex plant to ensure continued public access. This photograph looks south from Davenport toward the sea cliffs and pocket beaches of Coast Dairies State Park. (Photograph by Ed Dickie.)

DAVENPORT PIER, 2008. Sculpted Monterey cypress line the cliff above remnants of the old Davenport Portland Cement Company pier. The pier was closed in the 1950s due to storm damage and improvements in overland trucking. This is a dangerous beach to access, but that has not held back thousands of new visitors since the Davenport bluffs were opened to the public. (Photograph by Ed Dickie.)

SAN VICENTE CREEK TUNNEL, 2008. This diversion project was created when railroad construction necessitated a dirt fill across the San Vicente Creek estuary. This tunnel provides the creek an outlet to the ocean and has performed well for over 100 years despite some initial doubts. The opening is on Davenport's main beach and is the southern boundary for endangered coho salmon. Arthur Taylor, the editor of the *Daily Surf* in Santa Cruz, commented, "The San Vicente Creek, beloved of the angler and the artist, has its mouth stopped by a vast dike, and its throat choked into a tunnel, a saloon on its border, and its bed for miles denuded of the granite cobbles and sand beds. A sawmill is swiftly cutting out the timber and dirt and debris defile the pools and clog the riffles where lurked the gamey trout." (Photograph by Ed Dickie.)

NEW FORESTERS HALL, 2009. The old Foresters Hall was torn down and rebuilt by local George Majors. The bottom floor was occupied for three years by the Davenport Art Gallery. Randall Graham's Bonny Doon Vineyard took over in 2013 and opened a tasting room. Graham is known for championing grapes from the Rhône Valley. In 1991, the "Rhoneranger" asteroid was named in his honor. A flashing rocket ship once pierced the upper-deck roof. (Photograph by Ed Dickie.)

AMGEN TOUR OF CALIFORNIA BIKE RACE, 2009. This international Tour de France–style race was routed through Davenport in February 2009. The road from Santa Cruz to Davenport gets on the route of races like Amgen and the Santa Cruz Triathlon partly because it is both a beautiful and challenging ride. Ferrari, Porsche, and Corvette car clubs meet regularly in Davenport. (Photograph by Ed Dickie.)

COMMUNITY GATHERING, 2010.
Having turned 100 years old in 2015, the St. Vincent de Paul Church continues its tradition of offering weekend Catholic masses both in English and Spanish and providing a public space for seasonal events. DOM, inscribed on many Italian churches, is from a Latin phrase, *Deo optimo maximo*, which roughly translates as "to God, most good, most great." Pictured is a Cinco de Mayo celebration organized by the DRSC. (Photograph by Ed Dickie.)

SWANTON BERRY FARM STAND, 2019.
Swanton Berry Farm was founded in 1983 by Jim Cochran and Mark Matze. Visitors to the farm stand can pick their own strawberries and enjoy soups, jams, and strawberry shortcake. Highlights for the farming operation over the years include becoming the first organic farm in California as well as the first organic farm to sign a contract with the United Farm Workers, AFL-CIO. Cochran is well known for his research into organic strawberry farming. (Photograph by Ed Dickie.)

RODONI FARMS PUMPKIN PATCH, 2010. First-generation Italian American Dante Rodoni began farming Brussels sprouts in 1935. He was an innovator and helped develop mechanical sorting and harvesting machines. In 1978, his son Mario took over the farm and still farms today with his two sons. In 2019, there were 65 acres of certified organic crops, including sprouts, leaks, artichokes, peas, beans, and of course, pumpkins. Pictured is the popular pumpkin patch south of Davenport. (Photograph by Ed Dickie.)

SLOW COAST, 2019. After walking the entire US Pacific Coast, author Wallace J. Nichols and family moved to the area and designated the section of coast north of Santa Cruz and south of Half Moon Bay "the Slow Coast." They operate the Slow Coast store behind the Davenport Roadhouse from an Airstream trailer. A portion of sales goes toward preserving oceans and forests and supporting communities. (Photograph by Ed Dickie.)

Ten

THE FUTURE IS NOW

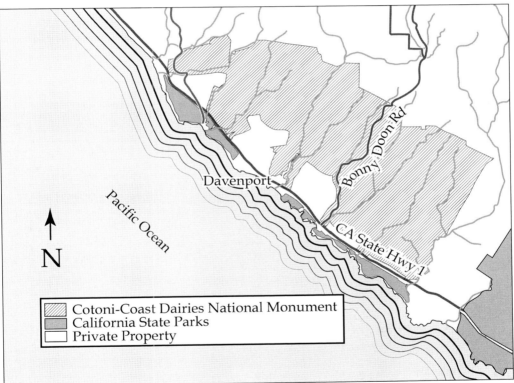

COAST DAIRIES LAND DISTRIBUTION MAP. The 7,000-acre Coast Dairies and Land Company property, which surrounds Davenport, was optioned for the development of luxury estates in the late 1990s, prompting the San Francisco conservation group Save the Redwoods League to negotiate a purchase. After the $40 million purchase, the property was transferred to the Trust for Public Land (TPL) of San Francisco. Included are six watersheds and more than seven miles of coastal resources, including beaches, agricultural lands, redwood forests, and endangered species habitat. (Courtesy of Sage Lee.)

COAST DAIRIES STATE PARK, 2012. TPL donated about 400 acres of Coast Dairies beaches to California State Parks in 2006, which created Coast Dairies State Park on the west side of Highway 1. The park includes Sharksfin, Bonny Doon, Yellow Bank (also known as Panther), and Laguna Creek Beaches. Pictured here are the beaches of Panther/Yellow Bank. The name "Yellow Bank" comes from the presence of oxidized iron in the rock, which makes the cliffs appear gold. (Photograph by Ed Dickie.)

COAST DAIRIES BENCHLANDS AND CLIFFS, 2009. In 2014, TPL transferred 5,600 acres to the Bureau of Land Management. This transfer includes land only to the east of Highway 1 and no beaches. TPL still holds the titles on the agricultural parcels and leases them out to local farmers. Designated as a boundary enlargement of the California Coastal National Monument, this federally managed land is now Cotoni-Coast Dairies National Monument. (Photograph by Ed Dickie.)

COTONI-COAST DAIRIES NATIONAL MONUMENT, 2014. This newly formed national monument contains important ethnobiological native food resources such as acorns, bay nuts, hazelnuts, buckeye, berries, and native grasses that were burned to cultivate grass seeds. This traditional territory is now associated with the Amah Mutsun Tribal Band, who are engaged in stewardship of this newly created national monument. (Courtesy of Michael Powers.)

SAN VICENTE FOREST, 2017. A consortium of local and national conservation groups purchased 8,532 acres from cement plant owner Cemex in 2011. Located east of Davenport, this is the largest privately owned parcel in Santa Cruz County. A portion of the second-growth forest will continue to be logged to fund restoration and recreation projects. Multi-use trails will connect to the Cotoni-Coast Dairies land, allowing for a skyline to sea trail experience. (Photograph by Ian Bornarth.)

NOT THE LAST TRAIN TO DAVENPORT, 2013. The Santa Cruz County Regional Transportation Commission completed the purchase of the Santa Cruz Branch Line from Union Pacific in 2012. As of 2019, plans to create a pedestrian and bicycle trail alongside the existing rail connecting Davenport to Santa Cruz are nearing completion. Pictured is a Sierra Northern train transporting machinery from the shuttered cement plant. (Photograph by Ed Dickie.)

LOOKING NORTH TOWARD DAVENPORT, 2013. Over 100 years of active land stewardship has been vital in preserving this world-class coast for the recreation-based visitation in modern times. Some beaches scarcely visited until now are energized with visitors seeking time on the sand and in the water. Hiking, biking, and equestrian opportunities are numerous. Current re-use studies for the 104-acre cement manufacturing facility suggest this rare coastal hamlet's story is just getting started. (Photograph by Ed Dickie.)

INDEX

DISCOVER THOUSANDS OF LOCAL HISTORY BOOKS FEATURING MILLIONS OF VINTAGE IMAGES

Arcadia Publishing, the leading local history publisher in the United States, is committed to making history accessible and meaningful through publishing books that celebrate and preserve the heritage of America's people and places.

Find more books like this at
www.arcadiapublishing.com

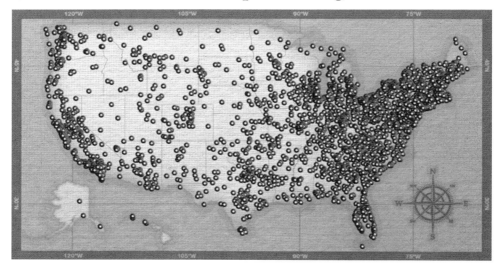

Search for your hometown history, your old stomping grounds, and even your favorite sports team.

Consistent with our mission to preserve history on a local level, this book was printed in South Carolina on American-made paper and manufactured entirely in the United States. Products carrying the accredited Forest Stewardship Council (FSC) label are printed on 100 percent FSC-certified paper.

MADE IN THE USA